Winning Grants to Strengthen Your Ministry

Winning Grants to Strengthen Your Ministry

Joy Skjegstad

THE
ALBAN
INSTITUTE

Herndon, Virginia
www.alban.org

The Alban Institute
2121 Cooperative Way, Suite 100
Herndon, VA 20171

Unless otherwise noted, all Scripture quotations are from the New Revised Standard Version of the Bible, copyright © 1989, Division of Christian Education of the National Council of the Churches of Christ in the United States of America, and are used by permission.

The Minnesota Common Grant Application Form (2000) in appendix A is reprinted with the permission of the Minnesota Council on Foundations, Minneapolis, Minn.

The material in appendix B from *Finding Common Ground: 29 Recommendations of the Working Group on Human Needs and Faith-Based and Community Initiatives* (2002) is reprinted with the permission of Search for Common Ground, Washington, D.C., from its Web site, www.sfcg.org.

Cover design by Adele Robey, Phoenix Graphics.

Library of Congress Cataloging-in-Publication Data

Skjegstad, Joy.
  Winning grants to strengthen your ministry / Joy Skjegstad ; foreword by Amy L. Sherman.
      p. cm.
  Includes bibliographical references.
  ISBN 978-1-56699-341-8
  1. Fund raising. 2. Church finance. I. Title.

  BV772.5.S55 2007
  254'.8--dc22
                                        2007008004

    12   11   10   09   08   07   UG   1   2   3   4   5   6

To Julia Grace Skjegstad Schrag,
the "bringer of light" in our lives.

Contents

Foreword

Several years ago I served as a grant reviewer for the Bush administration's first "Compassion Capital Fund," spending a week in Washington scrutinizing numerous grant proposals. The low point of the adventure came when I had to grade a lengthy proposal submitted by one faith-based organization on the Eastern Seaboard. Several trusted colleagues of mine knew of and had spoken highly of this group. Because of what I'd heard about the thoughtfulness of its leadership and the effectiveness of its programs, I longed to give it a top score—but couldn't. The proposal simply did not communicate the value of the organization. I reread the application four times, often muttering frustrated queries under my breath: "But what do you mean by this? But what did your initiative accomplish? But what is this expense item actually for?" All in all, too many "buts," resulting in one disappointing "if only"—if only this group had read a book like this one, maybe it would have enjoyed a substantial infusion of cash to support what, from all accounts I'd heard, was a promising enterprise.

I wish I could say that this experience was rare over the nearly two decades of my work with faith-based organizations (FBOs), but it's not. Like Joy Skjegstad, I've had the privilege of seeing scores of faith-based ministries up close and personal. The encounters are always interesting, often inspiring, typically uplifting, and sometimes disheartening because I sense that staff members are ill-equipped to articulate their story in a compelling and understandable way to donors that could support them. Many FBOs emerge from a local congregation, and the typical pastor or church worker has little or no formal training in fundraising or nonprofit management. This deficit has not stopped faith leaders from accomplishing significant achievements in community ministry, but it has often hindered them from effectiveness in raising funds from corporations and foundations. I will heartily commend *Winning Grants to Strengthen Your Ministry* to the faith leaders I meet, as it provides a comprehensive yet succinct and engaging guide to the steps needed to bridge that communications gap.

I suspect that many who purchase this book will do so with a certain air of resignation, akin to what most of us feel on the way to our six-month dental check-up: "I know I need this, but I'm not really looking forward to it." Ministry practitioners are usually "people persons"; what jazzes them up is the up-front contact with program participants, the hands-on opportunity to sow God's love in another's life and watch the exciting things that happen. Joy has done FBOs a service in this book by explaining how the work of fundraising is also ministry. If I have a word of advice to the reader, it's this: ministry didn't stop when you picked up this book, it's happening now as you read it. This book will help shape better thinking about how and why you do what you do. *And effective compassion ministry is very much a matter of the head as well as the heart.*

I've sometimes heard ministry leaders assert: "What matters most is faithfulness, not results." There's a measure of truth in that statement. After all, we can control our own behavior (choosing to be faithful) but we cannot determine, finally and exclusively, the transformation that occurs in others (program participants themselves, other people they may be connected to, and God all have influence here). The problem with this mind-set, though, is that it presumes we have no biblical responsibility to take all the steps we can to make positive change likely. That assumption flies in the face of biblical counsel to count the cost, to learn risk assessment, to be intentional and deliberate, to be sober-minded and hardworking, and to plan appropriately. Contrary to the bumper sticker's message, we are not called to "random kindness" or "senseless" acts of beauty. We are called to love—and to love well.

Loving well involves thinking well. It means taking the time to learn best practices and to seek out fruitful partnerships that can enhance our services. It means learning to focus our limited time and energies strategically; it means time spent in prayer, discussion, and discernment to clarify what God has called us to. It means stewarding well the resources we manage. In short, loving well involves intentionality and a considerable dose of discipline. For ministry leaders, it means sacrificing time not only on the front lines of ministry, face-to-face with people who hurt. It also requires some hours in the back office carefully estimating budgets and composing programming timelines, so that we don't overextend and let people down or run out of money, and thus fail to keep our promised services going.

I agree with what Joy has discovered in her own work with FBOs: one of the best exercises in learning to "think well" is writing grant proposals. This book can be your coach, laying out the activities you can complete that will help you, your staff, and your board think more clearly, more comprehensively, and more strategically about your important work. I hope it will help you win grants, and I believe the biggest winners from your investing your time digesting its advice will be the people you serve.

Amy L. Sherman
Senior Fellow, Sagamore Institute for Policy Research
Director, Center on Faith in Communities, Charlottesville, Virginia

Preface

It's 1987, and I have just taken my first management job in the nonprofit sector. I am 23 years old and the assistant director of a small church partnership that provides emergency food and financial assistance to families. At a meeting of community organizations, someone asks me whether our group wants some of the grant money that is available to help low-income families pay their utility bills. Being an intelligent young woman, I say "Yes!" Then they say: "To receive the money, you just need to go back to your office and write a grant proposal."

As I drove back to the office, I felt excited about the new money that was coming our way. I felt highly competent and wanted to tell my boss how wise he was to have hired me. But as I sat in my office and basked in my success, I had to ask myself: "What in the world is a grant proposal and how can I write one?"

Thus began my career in grantwriting. I have been doing it for nearly 20 years, and I am still learning. For me, the process of learning about grantwriting has included a great deal of trial and error in understanding how funders think, how to put together a winning proposal, and in the end, how not to take the outcome personally. I have learned to love the process of writing grant proposals, and I recommend it to anyone as a way to sharpen thinking about ministry and to draw out stories that need to be told.

My main reason for writing this book is that I am passionate about the role that faith-based groups play in communities and want to do everything I can to help ministry organizations succeed. I have been privileged to work with hundreds of ministry groups over the years, first as a church employee and now as a ministry consultant. I am continually amazed by the creative and effective approaches used by ministry groups, often to help people who have been rejected by their families, their communities, and even other nonprofits. I have come to believe that any discussion of social problems in this country needs to involve the faith community, because of the compassion, creativity, and knowledge about community needs that ministry leaders possess.

Miscommunication and misunderstanding still exist between some secular funders and ministry groups. The lack of a common language is a real problem in potential funder/ministry partnerships. At times, I've watched conversations quickly become difficult because the people representing the funders and the ministries didn't know how to talk with each other. More work needs to be done in both the philanthropic and ministry communities to broaden awareness of how and why faith-based groups can be funded. I've included tools in this book to help ministries communicate with secular funders, and I hope these will help make funder/ministry conversations easier and more productive.

You'll notice that I do not explicitly cover the writing of proposals for government grants in this book. I decided that seeking government grants for ministry is a complex and specialized field that deserves its own book. And because my specialty has been writing proposals for corporate and foundation grants, I decided my book should focus on that. Also, a note about two terms I use. "Funder" is a generic term used to describe a giving institution such as a foundation or corporation. "Grantwriting" is used throughout the book as a shortening of the phrase "grant proposal writing."

My hope is that this book brings clarity to ministry leaders about how and whether to seek corporate and foundation funding for their ministries. In my experience, ministry groups are less experienced than other types of nonprofit organizations in discerning which grant funding to seek, understanding how to build relationships with funders, and putting together proposals. I've seen this inexperience prevent some great ministry ideas from moving forward. I've seen passionate ministry leaders become discouraged because they couldn't find the resources they needed for their ministry. On the other side, I've watched ministry groups enter into relationships with funders that weren't a good fit for them, meaning that the ministry had to deal with difficult reporting requirements or pressure from a funder to leave the faith aspect of their programs behind. I hope that this book helps to "level the playing field" for ministry organizations, providing tools and insight that will make foundation and corporate funding more accessible to them.

I hope you feel encouraged as you read this book. There's a lot of information here, and it may seem overwhelming at times. Just know that grantwriting is an ongoing process, whether you are new to it or have been doing it for years. I'm in my 20th year of grantwriting, and I am still learning. I hope this book helps to make the process smoother and more enjoyable for you, and ultimately fruitful for your ministry.

Acknowledgments

A number of people consented to be interviewed for this book. I am grateful to them for taking time away from their piles of grant proposals.

Erika Binger, chair of the board, the McKnight Foundation
Heather Elting-Ballard, freelance grantwriter
Karol Emmerich, president, Emmerich Family Foundation
Chris Ganzlin, program director, and Karen Sciortino, program associate, the McKnight Foundation
Karen Kelley-Ariwoola, vice president, Community Philanthropy, the Minneapolis Foundation
Ellen Luger, executive director, General Mills Foundation
David Nasby, retired General Mills executive
Helen Tygret, grant development consultant
Elsa Vega-Perez, program officer, Otto Bremer Foundation

I used information from the interviews by quoting people directly (though anonymously) or by noting that the point I make is based on what funders or fundraisers have said to me. The rest of the material in this book is based on my 20 years of grantwriting experience and the opinions I have developed on the topic as a result.

In writing this book, I drew heavily on my experiences as a grantwriter for several nonprofit organizations. I am grateful for the opportunities I was given, particularly early in my career, to learn grantwriting on the job. A special thank-you to the staff and members of both Park Avenue United Methodist Church and Sanctuary

Covenant Church, two congregations in Minneapolis where I served on staff and learned a great deal about how God is working in the city and providing resources for that work. Special thanks as well to Church of the Open Door, also in the Twin Cities area, where I was given new opportunities to speak, and where I continue to learn much about following the leading of the Holy Spirit

I must also thank the people I worked with at TURN (Twin Cities Urban Reconciliation Network) and the Center for Non-profit Management at the University of St. Thomas, both in Minneapolis/St. Paul, where I taught ministry leaders about nonprofit management, including grantwriting. This book came out of some initial ideas I developed while directing the Institute for Ministry Leaders, a collaboration of TURN and the university.

I have worked with my editor, Beth Gaede, on two books now and continue to be grateful to her for being both persistent and kind. And my reviewers, who provided invaluable feedback as I was polishing my manuscript, are inspiring and dedicated nonprofit leaders: Joani Essenburg, Pat Peterson, and Chanda Smith.

I have two friends who walk faithfully with me through my life and who have been an encouragement to me as I worked on the book. I owe much to Shanni, for always turning me back to God, and to Jen, for going on this journey with me.

I owe a great deal to my father, Arnold Skjegstad, who taught me to love the church at an early age. Dad became a Christian later in life and has been a devoted supporter of the church ever since, giving tirelessly to further many ministries. Now 86, he continues to teach me that church is worth it, even when it's hard.

Finally, I owe much to my own family for their ongoing support and encouragement: to my children, Julia and Ethan, who inspire me with their energy and questions, and to my husband, Brad, who goes with me wherever God calls me, even if it's risky and hard. Thank you for your patience, wisdom, and love.

1

Faith and Fundraising: Can They Go Together?

"I wanted to go into ministry, not fundraising. I want to teach and comfort the people, not talk to them about money all the time."

Can faith and fundraising go together? You can probably guess my answer to this question. Yes! It's important to think about the fit between faith and fundraising before diving into the fund-seeking process, because the messages we get from our culture (and often within our churches) contradict the idea that money and ministry go together. Fundraising should be an integral part of the ministry: it can force us into deeper conversation with God and into relationships with others. It can build both faith and discipline. To push fundraising off to the side or to disconnect it from the rest of ministry is to limit how God can work in us and the people we are working to serve.

One of the best places to start in considering faith and fundraising is to look at the differences between the cultural messages we get about money (both inside and outside the church) and what God has to say. Aligning ourselves with a "kingdom of God" view of money will prepare us to make fundraising a fruitful part of the ministry.

In the kingdom of God, money is not the point, and we need to guard ourselves against letting it become our number-one concern or the essence of our identity. We are warned throughout the Bible not to let money take over our lives. At the same time, money is identified as a tool that can be used for good. Among many of Jesus's teachings on the topic of money, he teaches us not to "store up for yourselves treasures on this earth," because "where your treasure is, there your heart will be also" (Matt. 6:19, 21). Once we develop this kingdom view of money and it takes the proper place in our lives, we can begin to use money as a tool to help others and to accomplish God's purposes on earth. In my work with ministry groups, I hear many "kingdom of this world" views of money that I think contradict what God has in mind. One of the most common views of ministry fundraising is often framed as a question: should I have to ask for the money, or will God just provide it?

Should I Have to Ask for the Money?

Frequently people in ministry say something like this to me: "I don't think I should have to go around and ask people for money for our ministry. God will put it on someone's heart to give to us, and then we'll have all of the resources we need."

I call this the "manna" method of fundraising. People who use this approach believe that the money will just be lying on the lawn each day, and all we have to do is go out with a basket and pick it up. In one of my executive director jobs, I would often dream at night about picking up the money off the lawn. Gathering the money God dropped on us seemed so much easier than having to chip away at my fundraising tasks every day.

Despite my own dreams about it, I think this common view of securing ministry resources is limited and incorrect. The "manna" method of fundraising assumes that God immediately provides everything required for any good ministry idea. This conception isn't accurate. I've seen many great ministry ideas fall by the wayside over the years owing to lack of funds. And I've seen some ineffective ministries with questionable theologies raise tons of dough. This inequity causes me to ask: "What gives, God?" I still don't know why this seeming injustice persists in funding patterns, but I have learned that receiving funds isn't necessarily a sign of God's blessing. Also, the lack of funding doesn't necessarily mean that God disapproves of a particular ministry. In Matthew 5:45, Jesus says that God "sends rain on the righteous and the unrighteous." It is also true that "the money falls on the just and the unjust."

The expectation that we shouldn't have to ask for money contradicts the view of community and relationships presented throughout the Bible. God calls us to be in relationship with others, and asking people for financial resources is one way we build those relationships. Paul, in his many letters to the churches he ministered to, was not shy about describing financial needs and asking particular people to help with them. Paul's letters offer a complete view of the community that the church is supposed to be. We are to care for each other, work to meet needs, and be in authentic relationship. Paul describes the giving and securing of resources as an important part of the forming of a Christian community in which all give as they are able, contributing their skills, material resources, and ideas to the whole.

God calls us to work hard and exercise discipline in the work he has given us. Fundraising is difficult, often uncomfortable work, but that doesn't mean that we shouldn't have to do it. I've heard people in ministry describe fundraising as such a punishing task that they can't believe God would expect them to have to do *that*. Usually people feel this way because they believe they lack the expertise, courage, or patience to complete the assignment. God often gives assignments that seem impossible to us, however. Think of the many examples in the Bible of huge and difficult tasks that God gave people to do. Noah suffered his neighbors' ridicule as he built a huge boat in the middle of dry ground. Nehemiah faced threats from his detractors as he led the rebuilding of the holy city that had fallen into ruin. Obedience and dependence on God enabled these two leaders to accomplish their difficult work.

Other "Kingdom of This World" Views about Money

Faith and fundraising can fit together in ministry, but in addition to the "manna" view, many other cultural attitudes about money keep faith and fundraising apart. Often the church reinforces these cultural views about money rather than challenging them. It is important to spot these beliefs and to ask God to root them out, so we can put fundraising in its proper place in our ministries. Here is my list of cultural views and attitudes about money I have had to wrestle with in my years of ministry. You may think of others.

Money is a sign of success

Are well funded ministries more "successful"? It's easy to start believing that, because a strong message within American culture tells us that when it comes to money, more is better. I have worked with ministry leaders who would never judge individual people by how much money they had but who were willing to judge ministry organizations that way.

The "name it and claim it" theology that has gained in both popularity and controversy in recent years is related to the view that money is a sign of success. The positive aspect of "name it and claim it" is that it causes people to aspire to something positive for themselves and then to ask God for it. I become concerned, however, when people focus on financial prosperity as the ultimate goal of life and ministry, and then begin to believe that they *deserve* financial success. God doesn't bestow or withhold blessing through the flow of money to our ministries. Rather, God offers us blessings by helping us grow into the people he has made us to be, living fully in our gifts and abilities whether or not we happen to be financially prosperous.

I think that looking first (and perhaps only) at the dollar signs in our ministries can be distracting, drawing us away from where God is working. If we follow the ministry model of Jesus, we see that success has little to do with the money. Success is measured by faithfulness, love, and service. Small ministries or people of modest means may be successful by the standards Jesus employed. Keep this in mind as you evaluate your own success in fundraising and as you develop relationships with other ministries.

People's worth depends on how much money they have (or give)

I never thought that I would value wealthy people more than people of more modest means, but I found myself sliding into this belief early in my fundraising career. I felt more grateful to bigger donors, since their large gifts helped lighten my fundraising load. But God kept bringing to my mind the passage about the widow and her mite. She was a donor, perhaps the smallest donor of all, but Jesus held her up as someone to emulate. That's the opposite of the usual cultural message we get that people's value is based on the amount of their wealth. Jesus identified the widow's faithfulness and sacrifice as the greatest gifts she gave: "Truly I tell you, this poor widow has put in more than all those who are contributing to the treasury. For all of them have contributed out of their abundance; but she out of her poverty has put in everything she had, all she had to live on" (Mark 12:43–44). As you move forward into ministry fundraising, get into the practice of being thankful for all of your donors, regardless of the amount of money each one gives.

Money should never be talked about in public

In this "full disclosure" American culture, it's still considered taboo to talk in too much detail about financial matters. People don't like to talk about their salaries, their net worth, how they spend their money, or what causes they give to. It's unfortunate, but the church often adopts this cultural view about "money-talk," even though money was a common topic for Jesus. I've been in some church circles where people were willing to talk about the most intimate details of relationships and family life, but they were shocked when I started talking about personal finances and giving.

Embracing the prevailing cultural view about money-talk makes it difficult to put finances, giving, and fundraising in the proper ministry perspective. If the norm in the church is never to speak about money, it will be difficult to develop more biblical, kingdom-of-God views on the subject. Refusing to speak about money also hinders ministry fundraising by making it challenging to ask for money. In my experience, change in this area comes through Christian leaders who are willing to talk openly about money from the pulpit, in small-group settings, and one-on-one. Change can also happen through ministry fundraising that encourages people to talk openly and productively about their money and what they do with it.

Whoever gets the money first wins

It's a "dog eat dog" world out there when it comes to money, and competing with each other to get the sale, make the investment, and earn the bonus is standard behavior. You'll find this same competitive spirit in the nonprofit sector with regard to fundraising, but I have come to question whether it belongs in ministry life.

When I started my first paid ministry job, I felt I was competing against other ministries that were also trying to raise money. But over time, I began to think differently, picturing other ministries as part of the larger family of God, our brothers and sisters or cousins who are working toward the same goals. I also began to develop an attitude of abundance, believing that God could release the resources for all of the ministries, and that someone else's fundraising success didn't necessarily interfere with our ability to raise money. Rather than writing off other ministries as competitors, I decided instead that I might consider partnering with them or offering advice or encouragement. In their book *Growing Givers' Hearts: Treating Fundraising as a Ministry,* Thomas H. Jeavons, general secretary of the Philadelphia Yearly Meeting of the Religious Society of Friends, and Rebekah Burch Basinger, a fundraising and stewardship consultant, describe the positive attitude toward "competitors" that Christian fundraisers can develop:

> If . . . fundraisers truly accept the promise of God's great abundance, it is no threat when the Christian organization down the street receives a magnificent gift. The fundraisers can relax in the confidence that comes with knowing that there is plenty more where the other gift came from. They can rejoice that God has touched someone's heart to evoke such generosity for a good cause. In fact, if the ultimate end for which a development team strives is the building up of God's people and the advancement of God's many ministries, fundraisers can and will see gifts that come to other Christian organizations as a triumph for all who view their work in development as ministry.[1]

What a beautiful picture of how we might rejoice when other ministries succeed in fundraising!

Learning that Fundraising Is Part of the Ministry

In my many years of work with ministry groups and other nonprofits, I've seen that fundraising is often the most difficult aspect of the work for board members and staff to embrace. Too often, we think of fundraising as something dirty that happens over in the corner, apart from the work of the ministry, as though today we are doing ministry—counseling people, feeding the hungry, and worshiping God—and then tomorrow we will step away from that ministry work to meet with donors and write some grant proposals. To do our very best work for God, we have to stop practicing this dichotomy and develop another way of thinking.

Fundraising is a part of the ministry that God calls us to, not separate from it. When we begin to see that asking for money is a part of what God desires us to do, we free ourselves from the cultural baggage and guilt that binds many of us. I have met many ministry leaders who experience a kind of paralysis when it comes time to talk about money, as though they were bound up by cultural messages like the ones described above. The voice in your head may say, "It's not nice to talk about money," for example, but this message doesn't come from God. There are too many instances in the Bible where money and the securing of resources for ministry are talked about openly. Money was a common topic for Jesus. When we give up our cultural baggage and guilt about money, we experience a new freedom, allowing us to grow spiritually ourselves and minister more effectively to others.

We can pray more freely about our fundraising activities

Ask God to show you how to find funders, write to them, and talk with them, and your attitude about fundraising will change. I can't guarantee that you will win every grant as a result, because sometimes

God's response to our requests is "No" or "Wait." But I can tell you, from personal experience, that your heart will change.

We can minister to funders, even secular ones

We usually don't think about foundation and corporate folk as part of our ministry universe (at least there was a time when I didn't), but the truth is that everyone we come into contact with brings opportunities to talk about matters of faith. When I began to think about funders as people with needs, issues, and questions about faith (just like everyone else), I began to have conversations with funders about their own faith journeys.

We can free other people to use their abilities and spiritual gifts

Many people live out their true calling by giving to others. In the church we call this the spiritual gift of giving—a deep generosity that comes from God. Failing to ask others to give is denying them the opportunity to exercise their gift, to be the people God has called them to be. I didn't truly understand this idea until I married my husband, Brad, who has a strong spiritual gift of giving. It is simply unnatural for him not to give. So rather than thinking that you are bothering people by asking them for money, think instead of freeing them to use the gifts that they have been given.

We can allow God to adjust our own attitudes about money

There's no quicker way to find out about your own baggage and beliefs regarding money than to start asking other people to give you some. I have often gone through a painful process of watching my own stereotypes and fears about money rise to the top of me where I could see them. Facing these beliefs was an unpleasant experience at first, but when I knew what my misshapen beliefs were, I could ask God to change my thinking and heal me. For example, as I mentioned earlier, I realized after a few years of fundraising that I was beginning to value people on the basis of how much money they had. This attitude is in direct contradiction to the way Jesus lived his life. I had to begin talking to God on a regular basis about how I came to be this way and how I could change.

Great Fundraisers of the Bible

To embrace this idea that fundraising is a part of the ministry, look into the Bible and reflect on how fundraising fits into the picture of God's work. I thought I would have to look pretty hard to find fundraising examples in the Bible; I was amazed to find that a number of biblical passages describe how resources were secured for the work of the Lord.

I think God wants us to see that securing the resources is one part of the work he calls us to. The biblical examples I include here describe resource-gathering as a part of the whole process of ministry. It is not highlighted as a separate or difficult or more important part of the work. But it is identified as part of it. These examples can help release us from the idea that identifying needs and asking for resources have no place in ministry. I offer this disclaimer, however: I don't think these passages necessarily provide guidance on the specific fundraising techniques we should use. For example, I don't think we should "plunder the Egyptians" (see Exod. 12) to raise support for our ministries.

Meeting needs in the early church

The early church was a community of believers who felt called to share everything in common. Because community members were so close to each other, I imagine that needs within the community were obvious to all. The early church raised resources to meet these needs by relying on its wealthiest members to sell their houses and lands and to contribute the funds. These first Christians weren't embarrassed to talk about needs and weren't shy about asking for money, as described in the following passage:

> There was not a needy person among them, for as many as owned lands or houses sold them and brought the proceeds of what was sold. They laid it at the apostles' feet, and it was distributed to each as any had need.

Acts 4:34–35

In the early church, the donors weren't lauded as more important than anyone else in the community. Their gifts are described as
one aspect of the way the community functioned.

Paul raises funds for missionary journeys and the poor

Paul was a bold preacher and missionary, and was bold in his fundraising activities as well. Throughout Paul's writings, we find reference to the raising of resources for his missionary journeys, as well
as the practice of collecting funds for the needy in Jerusalem.

The "collection for the saints" is described at the beginning
of 1 Corinthians 16, where Paul provides specific instructions on
how and when the church in Corinth is to collect the funds for the
Jerusalem Christians who are living in poverty. We get the impression that this collection has become standard practice for many of
the Christian churches; the church in Galatia is also mentioned in
this passage. The churches in Macedonia and Achaia are mentioned
in Romans 15. Paul writes a pointed reminder to the church at
Corinth in 2 Corinthians 8 and 9 about following through on a
"pledge" to help the poor:

> So I thought it necessary to urge the brothers to go on ahead to
> you, and arrange in advance for this bountiful gift that you have
> promised, so that it may be ready as a voluntary gift and not as
> an extortion.

> 2 Corinthians 9:5

Paul is unafraid to use strong language to remind the Corinthians about keeping the promise they made to take up an offering for
the poor. Paul's writings also contain references to support raised
for his own ministry, though he is less bold in asking for his own
support than in asking for funds for the poor. Philippians 4 contains
a heartfelt thank-you to the Philippian church for its monetary support of his work:

> You Philippians indeed know that in the early days of the gospel,
> when I left Macedonia, no church shared with me in the matter

of giving and receiving, except you alone. For even when I was in Thessalonica, you sent me help for my needs more than once.

Philippians 4:15–16

This is just one of many places in Paul's writings that include a description of sharing resources to meet needs within the community of believers.

Nehemiah rebuilding the walls of Jerusalem

The story of Nehemiah is one of my favorites in the Bible, because it is inspiring to read about his courage in the face of a seemingly hopeless situation: the need to rebuild the walls of Jerusalem. After studying this story many times, I started to notice that Nehemiah was not afraid to ask specifically for what he needed to do the job. In the second chapter, we see him ask his employer (the king of Persia) for the letters of recommendation and the raw materials he needed to rebuild the wall of Jerusalem.

> Then I said to the king, "If it pleases the king, let letters be given me to the governors of the province Beyond the River, that they may grant me passage until I arrive in Judah; and a letter to Asaph, the keeper of the king's forest, directing him to give me timber to make beams for the gates of the temple fortress, and for the wall of the city, and for the house that I shall occupy."

Nehemiah 2:7–8

Raising the resources is described in a matter-of-fact way in Nehemiah's story—one of many steps he took to accomplish this difficult task.

Israelites leaving Egypt

On the way out of Egypt, the Israelites are instructed by Moses to "plunder the Egyptians." God gives the Israelites favor, and the Israelites make their exodus possessing jewelry and clothing that had belonged to their captors. I have always wondered whether this release of resources was part of God's provision for the Israelites' journey into freedom. Having been slaves, it's unlikely they had the resources or material goods to make the journey, and the Egyptian plunder might have provided clothing and funding they needed. Of course, some of the jewelry they took ended up in the Golden Calf, but that is another story. The Israelites followed their leader into asking the least likely funders of all for resources:

> The Israelites had done as Moses told them; they had asked the Egyptians for jewelry of silver and gold, and for clothing, and the Lord had given the people favor in the sight of the Egyptians, so that they let them have what they asked. And so they plundered the Egyptians.
>
> Exodus 12:35–36

God performed a miracle for the Israelites by giving them favor with their oppressors, providing much-needed resources.

Integrating Faith and Fundraising

I encourage you to spend some time reflecting on your views of fundraising and ministry and consider how these can be better aligned with what we know about God's views on those topics. Then you'll be ready for the next step, which is to work on integrating faith and fundraising into your ministry, applying the concepts described previously in this chapter.

On the organizational level, it's important to outline how faith influences your fundraising approaches. What are the key principles and scriptural passages that influence how you operate? How do these scriptures and principles affect your approach to fundraising? For example, if one of your principles is to value all donors, giving no one preferential treatment based on the size of a gift, how would that affect your fundraising approaches? Would you decide to expand your invitation list for the annual donor recognition dinner as a response?

Identifying how faith and fundraising fit together in your organization could become a part of your strategic-planning processes. For example, the "values" section of your strategic plan could include values about fundraising practice. All of the people involved in or overseeing fundraising activities for your ministry should take part in this discussion, so that everyone can operate from the same principles when they are representing your ministry to donors. Your fundraising values might include statements like these:

- Our ministry won't take money from companies that create products that are harmful to our community.
- Our ministry will value all donors equally, regardless of how much or how little money they give.
- Our ministry will not exploit the people we serve to raise money.

Putting your values into practice by developing specific strategies is important too. Develop a fundraising plan that identifies strategies to be used, targeted dollar amounts, and a list of tasks to be completed by whom and when.

Faith and fundraising need to be integrated not only on the organizational level, but on a personal level as well. You will find that integrating faith and fundraising into your own life will require you constantly to cultivate a generous heart. A generous heart values people, not money. A generous heart refuses to view other people as adversaries or enemies. As people of faith, we should strive to be generous to others in our actions, words, and attitudes. When fundraising decisions don't go our way, it can be easy to develop a less-than-generous attitude toward donors, potential donors, and other ministries and their staff members. In my experience, this lack of generosity can come on gradually, and before you know it, you have developed a full-blown bad attitude. That's why it is important to keep cultivating a generous heart, one that reflects kingdom-of-God values by making sure that we minister both to those who give us funds and those who choose not to.

Being disciplined in your relationship with God through Scripture study and prayer is critical to the development of a generous heart. These practices, and others that your tradition may use, can help you hear God's voice as you work to raise money. Being in community with other Christians is also important, whether that community is formed through a congregation, a small group, or an accountability or spiritual-direction relationship. People I'm in community with have confronted me when I have developed a bad attitude toward someone and am acting less than generous. Their honesty has forced me to work harder on keeping a generous heart, even in situations where it was difficult.

I've put this chapter first because your faith is the groundwork for your fundraising, the most important thing to consider as you develop fundraising values and strategies. Keeping the faith so that you pursue principles and values, rather than money, power, or "success" as defined by our culture, is critical as you raise funds for ministry. Integrating faith and fundraising is something to be worked at constantly, as you identify your own cultural beliefs, follow spiritual disciplines, and cultivate your generous heart.

Key Questions

1. What cultural views do you have about money that make it difficult to fit faith and fundraising together? What can you do to overcome these views?

   _____

   _____

   _____

   _____

2. Who are your favorite fundraisers of the Bible? Why?

   _____

   _____

   _____

   _____

3. What Scripture passages are important to you as you work to fit faith and fundraising together?

   _____

   _____

   _____

   _____

4. What spiritual practices can you adopt to develop a generous heart?

   _____

   _____

   _____

   _____

2

Are Grants Right for Your Ministry?

"The ministry at our youth center is growing. Do you think the First Corporation Foundation would give us a grant?"

"We need to get some grant money to expand our church building."

"We need to add a new pastor to the staff. Could we get grant money for that?"

You bought this book because you have wondered whether grant funding is available for your ministry and, if so, how you can get it. The answer to this question is, "It depends." I talk with hundreds of people in ministry each year, most of whom have the idea that grants to fund their ministries are available somewhere out there, it's just a matter of finding them. This idea may or may not be true.

Whether your ministry is fundable by grants depends on a number of factors, including:

- how closely your mission matches the funder's mission (the most important factor);
- whether your ministry collaborates with any other organizations;
- the results that your programs achieve;
- the extent to which your ministry is faith-based and how the funder feels about that;
- whether your programs are innovative;
- the financial soundness of your organization;
- the qualifications of your staff and volunteers.

17

Whew! That's quite a list! This book will help you think through these factors as you work to prepare your grant proposal. First, though, you need to decide whether grant funding is right for your ministry and if so, if you are ready to apply for grants now.

An Overall Funding Picture

I hear it all the time: "I want a big grant for my ministry so that I don't have to keep raising money all of the time." The very best thing for your ministry is exactly the opposite—to find many kinds of funding in various amounts. This concept is counterintuitive for most of us. Fundraising is hard for the average person, so most people long for the one or two big gifts that would make the need to raise funds go away, at least for a while. What you should be working toward instead is a broad funding base that includes grants as just one part of a larger funding picture. The best fundraising programs I have been a part of included not only grants but also contributions from individual donors, special events, and church partners, as well as in-kind gifts.

One advantage of a broad funding base is that your organization will be much less affected if large gifts are not renewed. If certain types of donations decline, other kinds of gifts can buoy up the organization until you have the opportunity to develop new strategies and new donors. For example, some corporate gifts may decline as certain types of employers struggle or reposition themselves in the economy—witness the spate of bank mergers a few years back, for example. Your organization will be in a much better position to weather this storm if you have already developed a base of giving through individuals, private foundations, churches, and special events.

I offer some tips below on how you might go about raising some of these "non-grant" funds for your ministry. Look at the list on the following pages, "Elements of a Broad Support Base," to get a sense of the many types of funding you could seek for your ministry. Keep in mind as you read that it can take years to develop a broad (many types of sources) and deep (lots of money) funding base. You may decide to focus on just one or two of these fundraising

Elements of a Broad Support Base

Types of funders/donors

Individuals
Private foundations
Family foundations
Corporate foundations
Corporate giving programs
Government agencies
Small businesses
Churches
Service clubs

Types of cash gifts

Unrestricted or general operating
Program support
Capital gifts (for building projects or major equipment)
Endowment

Types of noncash gifts

In-kind donations (examples: printing or legal services, vehicles,
    computers)
Property
Insurance
Trusts
Planned, deferred gifts
Time, wisdom, talent

Earned income
(Sales of a product or service to benefit your organization)

Thrift-store goods
T-shirts

Books
CDs

Fund-raising Events

Golf tournaments
Fund-raising dinner/silent auction
Carnival
Concert

strategies for now, but I would recommend that you eventually broaden the number of strategies used.

Individual Donors

Developing a group of individuals who give to your organization is a great strategy, whether your group is new or has been around for years. In my opinion, this is the best kind of money for several reasons.

1. *Individual donors tend to give over a longer period of time than foundations or corporations.* If you keep your donors updated, and ask and thank them on a regular basis, you can expect many of them to stick with you over a period of years. Foundations and corporations, on the other hand, tend to change their focus every few years—and that may mean you won't be able to depend on grant funding over the long term.

2. *Individual donors may be less restrictive with their gifts than foundations or corporations.* It is becoming harder and harder to get unrestricted money from foundations and corporations, but many individual donors seem willing to give and to leave it up to you to decide how to use the money.

3. *Individual donors may be able to increase their gifts or give more often than a foundation or corporation can.* Once individual donors are "in your fold," you can cultivate them further, perhaps

developing the relationship to the point that you can ask for gifts more often and in larger amounts. Grantmaking organizations, on the other hand, typically give once a year and may not be in a position to expand the size of their gifts significantly, because of budget constraints or the sheer number of grant requests they receive in a year.

4. *Individual donors may draw other individual donors into relationship with your organization.* If you develop close relationships with your donors, particularly those who make larger gifts, you may be in a position to ask them to invite other donors to give to your group.

5. *Individual donors can help build ties with potential corporate funders.* Some of your donors may work for companies that make grants, and those companies might make a grant to your ministry if the donor puts in a good word for you. Also, some companies match employee donations to charity, meaning that your donors who are corporate employees could multiply their gifts, perhaps several times over.

I have worked on a number of individual donor campaigns over the years. Here are a few tips based on my experience:

- Recruit board members who can help you with fundraising, people with a circle of influence that may include potential major donors.
- Develop "sponsorship packages" for donors—sponsoring a student or a classroom, a program, or a new initiative. Individual donors respond well to opportunities that pinpoint a particular need or opportunity.
- Communicate with your donors regularly, updating them on successes and opportunities.
- Be sure to include "response devices" (a pledge card and an envelope) when communicating with donors by mail. Fewer people will give if you make it hard for them to respond.
- Remember that some individual donors like to give in ways that don't involve just sending a check in the mail. Some donors may give your group noncash gifts such as property, stocks, or bonds. These can be sold, and the cash used to move your ministry forward. Other donors may choose to

defer their gifts through planned-giving options that transfer assets to your organization after the donor's death. The simplest way is for donors to include your group in their wills, but some donors may choose to use trusts or annuities to give to your ministry.

- Look for opportunities to present your ministry to groups with which your individual donors are affiliated, such as religious congregations, service clubs (like Rotary), and professional associations.

In-kind gifts

Donated goods or services can be just as valuable to your ministry as cash. Check with volunteers, board members, and people in partner congregations to see what types of donations they can find for you. You may find people who could donate:

Property
Athletic equipment
Printing services
Computer equipment and software
Vehicles
Legal services
A host of other products and services

One tip on accepting donated goods: before accepting them, always make sure that they are in good working order and are useful to you. Getting a bunch of donated shoes when you don't give away shoes doesn't help anyone. And if someone gives you computers that were new four or five years back, they probably won't work with today's software packages. Don't be afraid to say no to broken or useless items. You'll just waste your time getting rid of them.

Another tip: I always recommend that groups research any potential donations of property before accepting them. You don't want to find out about the leaking hazardous-waste dump underground or the unpaid back taxes after the property has been donated to you, because of the potential liability for your organization.

Fundraising events

Fundraising events can be a great addition to your fundraising program, garnering both money and visibility for your organization. However, keep the following tips in mind.

1. *Keep fixed costs low at the start.* One danger of fundraising events is that you may have to pay a great deal of money up front for fixed costs, without knowing how many people will attend.

2. *Get sponsors to cover your costs.* The most successful fundraising events have sponsors that cover the up-front, fixed costs of the event. That way, you will be assured that you won't lose money. Also, participants in the event can then be told that 100 percent of their donation (or ticket cost) will go directly to "Hands and Feet Ministry" or "Temple Youth Center." Sponsors are typically acknowledged in any publicity for the event and at the event itself.

3. *Build a strong committee to sell tickets (or tables, or foursomes, and so forth).* If your event is one that people will pay to participate in, be sure to develop a committee of people who have the connections to sell a lot of tickets. People won't come to an event because they see an ad in the newspaper or receive a mailing. They'll buy a ticket and attend because someone they know and respect invites them. That's the work of your event committee—getting as many people as possible to attend.

I worked on a golf tournament once with the owners of a local grocery chain. They invited all of their vendors, and you'd better believe that all of the people from the soap, chocolate, breakfast-cereal, and produce companies (to name just a few) showed up at the event. We made money on the tournament our very first year, because we had the right people inviting folk to participate in the event.

4. *Recruit volunteers who can help organize the event, managing the many details involved.* I know from personal experience that fundraising events are almost always more work than anticipated at the outset, so plan to have a number of extra hands around to handle the details. For small organizations in particular, there's always the danger that the executive director will end up devoting weeks and months to the details of a fundraising event. Involving

volunteers at all levels of event planning and implementation can help you avoid that pitfall.

Earned-income projects

This funding strategy involves creating income streams for your organization through the sale of products or services you produce. Many youth organizations sell T-shirts, for example, or perhaps your ministry sells books or tapes. Over the years, I've seen many earned-income projects succeed, and I've seen many fail. These seem to be the keys to success:

- Keep up-front costs low, at least at the start.
- Sell a product or service that people need to buy anyway, and it will be easier for them to make the switch to what you are selling to help out a ministry.
- Focus your sales efforts on "built-in" markets within your organization. These include members at partner churches, program participants and their families, donors, community groups you work with, and other collaborative partners. If you don't have to create a market for your products from scratch, you'll experience success sooner.

It takes years to build a fundraising program that includes all of these elements, but it's worth working toward. Start setting goals now to have a major fundraising event next year or the year after, for example, and you can begin to put the people and infrastructure in place to make it happen. Fundraising takes on an immediacy in many ministries that prevents long-term thinking. Instead, take the time to look forward a few years, and to develop a fundraising plan that includes many kinds of grants, individual donors, fundraising events, and earned-income projects.

Advantages of Grant Funding

You may think that the answer to the question "Do you want this grant?" is always yes. But yes may be the wrong answer, depending on the particular funder. Weigh the advantages and disadvantages of grant funding carefully each time you consider asking for a grant, and you'll end up with funders who are a good fit for your organization. In general, however, pursuing ministry funding through grants offers the following advantages.

1. *Grants can provide a large chunk of money early on in the life of a ministry.* It takes time to build a funding base for a ministry, particularly if you are doing it person-to-person with individual donors. I always advise ministries to pursue gifts from individual donors as a part of their fundraising picture. However, developing a solid funding base that way can take years. Fundraising events can take a long time to become successful as well, often needing to be run consistently for several years before they become moneymakers.

Grants, on the other hand, can provide a big chunk of money at one time. If you can meet a funder's guidelines and write a compelling proposal, you may be able to secure a significant amount of grant funding for your ministry in a relatively short period of time. I say "may," because there are never any guarantees in the grants business. (There's a lot more about that later in the book.)

Particularly if you are starting up or are a small organization, grant funding can help you leap forward in a short period of time, perhaps enabling you to add programs, staff, and infrastructure that the organization needs. This grant-fueled growth can give you some early success, enabling you to attract other funding as well.

2. *Grants provide a stamp of approval that may attract other donors to your ministry.* Once you've received funding from a foundation or corporation, it will be much easier to secure other grants. Your first grants can also help to attract the support of individual donors. When it comes to fundraising for nonprofits, money follows money.

One dynamic in the world of grantmaking: usually a few foundations and corporations are looked to by other funders as leaders in the field. If you can secure a grant from one of these "gatekeeper" funders, you have won a stamp of approval that indicates to other funders that you are doing something right.

Often gatekeeper funders are ones that have a more rigorous review process. In my own state of Minnesota, the McKnight Foundation, the largest private family foundation in the state, plays this role. Once you have received your McKnight grant (no small task), other funders take the attitude, "If they made it through the McKnight process, they must be worth consideration." You can find out which are the gatekeeper funders are in your area by talking with experienced fundraisers.

Other types of donors, including individuals and government agencies, may also be positively influenced once grant money starts flowing into your ministry. Getting grants can make your organization seem more substantial, indicating that you are doing something right and that you will probably be around for a while.

3. *Grants can be relatively "free" money.* If a staff member or volunteer can write a strong grant proposal for you, getting grant funding may cost much less up-front than some other funding options. For example, fundraising events and earned-income projects usually have up-front costs that require you to take a risk before you know how many tickets or T-shirts you'll sell. Some nonprofits use loans or other types of financing to underwrite their work, particularly if they are working in a field like housing that has many up-front costs. Getting a grant is typically a less expensive option than covering the fees and interest payments that accompany loans. A grant that covers all or most of a project at the outset also puts much less strain on an organization's budget over the long term than loan payments that may continue for years.

You may decide as an organization to seek outside help from a professional grant writer, in which case grantwriting may not be less expensive for you than other fundraising options, at least not at first. Experienced grant writers don't come cheap, but hiring one may be worth the expense for you. Grantwriting consultants can bring clarity to many issues quickly, creating a high-quality proposal that will get you further, faster in the world of foundations and corporations. Your best bet is to hire a grant writer with considerable experience who has worked with groups similar to yours and has the references to prove it. Many grant writers also have relationships with funders that may help you secure a grant. Grant writers cost more in the short term, but that investment will probably be worth it over the long term.

4. *Relationships with funders can lead to more than just a grant.* Some corporations and foundations like to provide their grantees

with a number of "extras" not available to groups that don't receive funding. As a grantee you may have access to:

- *Training and technical assistance paid for by the funder* (in full or in part) to help your organization move forward. There may be conferences, seminars, or one-on-one help regarding best practices in your field and organizational development, for example.
- *Networking with other grantees.* The funder may form a "cohort" of grantees in a particular area, providing opportunities to gather to share information, encourage each other, and even collaborate. One organization I worked for was invited into a roundtable of organizations providing after-school programming. The group got together once or twice a year to network and hear a special speaker on the topic. I found it helpful to compare notes with other groups doing similar work.
- *The expertise and knowledge of foundation staff members.* Foundation staff members often come to their positions from a particular field, such as early-childhood development or elder care. Being a grantee makes it easier to pick up the phone and consult with the staff on a variety of issues. Even if foundation staff members don't have the time or expertise to help you themselves, people in these positions usually have a bird's-eye view of the sector, with strong knowledge about who might be able to help you.

5. *Writing grant proposals forces you to get organized.* There's nothing like a grant deadline to force you to "get it all together." One of my ministry clients calls this the "cleansing process." Your organization may have been content to leave its mission, outcomes, and processes unclear and its program design rather vague. But most funding institutions won't tolerate that. Foundation and corporate funders expect you to be able to articulate, in specific terms, what your organization and its programs are all about.

Working through a set of grant guidelines and preparing your grant proposal may help you to:

- Clarify the mission and vision of your organization.
- Write down a detailed plan for your programs, including the types of activities to be offered, when they'll be offered, and who will carry them out.
- Set program outcomes and evaluation processes (a *big* deal to funders).
- Form program collaborations with other organizations.
- Develop a staffing plan, an organizational chart, and job descriptions.

Being able to clarify these issues will help your organization in many ways in addition to preparing you to seek funds. In my work as a grantwriting consultant, I find that working with my clients on defining programs and setting outcomes is often more important than the grant itself. When mission, vision, processes, and programs become more clearly defined, you will be able to move forward as an organization in new ways. Your staff, board members, and volunteers will better understand what they are supposed to be doing, and there may be a new sense of focus within the organization.

That said, sometimes you may need to let a grant deadline pass if you can't "get it together" fast enough. For example, if you don't have any collaborative partners for your program and the grant deadline is a month away, it will be difficult to build the needed relationships in so short a time. I once tried to put together a program collaboration for youth employment in a month to submit an application for a large grant. I don't recommend trying to do that.

Disadvantages and Challenges of Grant Funding

Sometimes I run into ministry leaders who talk about grants as though they will provide a magic cure for whatever ails their ministry. It's important to realize that grants aren't magic, and they definitely have their limitations and disadvantages.

1. *Grant funding is typically not long-term or permanent.* Foundation and corporate funders frequently change their minds about what is important to them. For example, new statistics might be

released on a particular issue in your state, and the funders might respond. Or when a crisis occurs, perhaps a natural disaster or sudden economic downturn, grant makers may turn their attention there and away from areas where their focus used to lie.

Funders change their minds for many reasons, and some you won't be able to anticipate. The first time I served as an executive director, we lost a major grant because the leaders of a corporate foundation that had supported our organization for years decided they wanted to focus on more "high-profile" groups. Translation: they wanted to get more PR for their foundation buck. I did not see that one coming!

This shift in the funder's focus means that the grant you received for the past two or three years may not be renewed. Funder guidelines (described in more detail in chapter 6) describe the focus areas of each funder as well as the things that are typically not funded. Grant funders may change the following about their guidelines:

- Geographic focus.
- Demographic focus (adopting a new focus on a particular ethnic group, for example).
- Issue areas (backing off an area where they have been working to pursue another).
- Types of grants they provide (typically general operating, program or capital).
- The size of organizations that they fund.
- Anything else they decide to change!

It's important to understand the often fickle nature of corporate and foundation funders as you put together your funding base and future plans for the organization. Just when you thought you had all the funding pieces put together, one or two grants fall out of the picture because funders change their focus. That's one reason it's good to have a broad funding base, with grants as just part of the picture. An experienced fundraiser I know likes to say that grant funding just buys you time so that you can figure out how to replace the grant money when it goes away. In my experience, that's true.

2. *Grantmaking organizations may challenge the faith component of your ministry.* Many grantmaking organizations are secular;
that is, they don't have an agenda of bringing people to faith. This
can create a tension for your organization if you do have a faith
component to your programming. Secular funders usually state that
they do not want to fund "proselytizing" or programs that are exclusively for members of a particular religious group.

If your ministry does have spiritual content, it can be difficult to
decipher what secular funders consider OK and what is unaccept-
able to them. Foundation staff members who are not involved in
faith communities or who don't come from a religious background
may have difficulty understanding the language you speak, or even
making the effort to try. I've seen a number of difficult scenarios:

- Funders steer completely clear of faith-based groups, because they assume that proselytizing or evangelism is always
  a part of the effort.
- Funders misread anything ministry groups say to them
  about spiritual programming or content, assuming that
  faith is forced on participants.
- Ministry groups refuse to seek support from any secular
  funders, assuming that funders would insist that faith be
  removed from the picture.
- And, worst of all, ministry groups try to bend the faith part
  of their mission to accommodate what a secular funder is
  looking for. If reaching out to people spiritually is a key goal
  for your organization, avoid compromising that important
  part of your mission just to get some money.

Approaching secular foundation and corporate funders doesn't
always lead to the tension I've described here, but you should be
prepared before you start the conversation for a discussion of the
faith aspect of your ministry. These conversations are easier if you've
made the effort beforehand to define the "faith" in your "faith-
based" organization clearly. In chapter 5 I provide tips on relating
to secular funders.

3. *Many grants are restricted and must be applied to just one
program.* More and more frequently, foundation and corporate
funders are focusing their giving on particular program priorities,

not on unrestricted general operating grants. That means you may be able to get a grant to cover the expenses of your after-school tutoring program, but you are less likely to get grant funding to pay for your office manager's salary, fundraising costs, or office rent. In other words, most grant funding has limitations in how it can be used to benefit your organization.

4. *The reporting required by grantmaking organizations can be burdensome.* Be sure you understand a funder's reporting requirements before you even apply for a grant. Most funders require a report from their grantees at the end of the grant period. Find out what that involves. A one- or two-page update is reasonable and common, and you will want to provide one even if it isn't required by the funder. Communicating your successes and challenges is an important part of building strong relationships with your corporate and foundation donors.

However, some funders' reporting requirements go far beyond a brief update. You may secure a grant from one of these foundations or corporations and then find out that you have to provide extensive monthly or quarterly updates, using detailed forms or formats. Some funders also require financial information so extensive that it may not be worth it for you to apply. My experience is that the greatest reporting burden comes with government grants, but some other funders expect a great deal from their grantees as well, even if the grants are small.

Readiness Checklist

Ministry leaders frequently ask me, "How do we know if we're ready to write a grant proposal?" I have prepared a checklist of elements that it are good to have in place before you start writing. You may decide to start before you have all of them in place. Just know that these are factors that will influence your chances of success.

1. *You have incorporated as a 501(c)3 organization.* Foundations and corporations are less and less likely to consider a grant proposal if the organization hasn't incorporated as a 501(c)3 nonprofit organization. Getting your legal status shows that you are

serious and forces your group to put governance and accountability structures into place. Your 501(c)3 status makes it less risky for a funder to support you.

Fewer and fewer funders will allow you to arrange for another 501(c)3 nonprofit to serve as your fiscal agent—that is, receive funds on your behalf. However, if you have already filed your federal application for nonprofit status and are simply waiting to hear from the IRS, some funders may be willing to consider a proposal from your group.

2. *You have someone working with you who has strong writing skills.* You don't necessarily need an experienced grant writer to prepare your grant proposals (though it certainly helps), but you do need someone who can write. Whether it's a staff member, volunteer, or consultant, you are looking for someone who can write up a compelling case for your organization, using clear, concise language. If your group needs to rely on volunteers to write the proposal, look for people who use writing as part of their profession. I've found that teachers and lawyers are often a good choice.

3. *You have vision and mission statements for your organization, even if they are informal.* Before submitting a grant, you should be able to write down, in just a couple of sentences, the vision and mission of your organization. A vision describes what the world will be like once your organization has completed its work: "all the children will be able to read" or "everyone in our community will have access to affordable housing," for example. A mission describes how your group will go about achieving the vision, addressing who, what, where, how, and with whom.

4. *Your program is functioning at some level.* Most corporate and foundation funders like to see a program in action before they send their support. If you are just starting your ministry organization, plan to have at least one program on the ground and running before you seek grant funds. It might be a small program run by volunteers, but having a track record and being able to demonstrate some early results will enhance your chances of getting grant funding.

5. *You have already raised some money for your ministry.* If your organization is new, grant money probably won't be the first money you secure. Foundations and corporations like to see that an organization has at least some support from elsewhere before they

make their commitments. They want to be assured that there is broad community support for the work and that the organization won't become too dependent on grant funding. Individual donors may be your first contributors, allowing your group to lay some groundwork. Churches have supplied seed money for several projects I have been involved in starting or restarting. We secured grant funding because we were able to start the project with the church seed money, then demonstrate initial results to corporate and foundation funders.

6. *You have a strong sense of how faith fits into your faith-based organization.* When you say you are a faith-based group, what does that mean to you? Most important, does being "faith-based" mean that some or all of your programs have a faith component with the goal of helping your participants grow spiritually? It's important to sort out that key point before you start applying to funders that may not have a spiritual bent at all. You don't want to get into a situation in which a funder is questioning you about the faith aspects of your programs and you have few answers.

If your group is fuzzy about how important the faith piece is and how it fits into your programs, I would recommend having a conversation within your organization (probably involving both board and staff) to discuss the issue. Keep in mind that some ministry organizations have a variety of programs, some with spiritual content and some without. In chapter 5 I detail the many ways of being faith-based and provide strategies for communicating with secular funders.

7. *Your programs have a clear design and focus.* This is often the sticking point with my consulting clients: they have formed their organization and started some programming, but their programs do not have a clear design. By clear program design I mean:

- You have identified a specific target audience that needs your program. (You can answer the question, who are your participants and what are their characteristics?)
- You have a well-defined set of activities. (You can answer the question, what, exactly, will you be doing?)
- You have a clear timeline for implementing those activities. (You can answer the question, when will the activities happen and how often?)

- You have a clear set of program outcomes and a way to measure them (You can answer the question, what will change in the lives of our participants as a result of our work?)
- You have identified who will be doing the work. (You can answer the question, which staff members or volunteers will be working on this?)

Funders can spot "fuzziness" on these issues a mile away. Coming up with the answers to the questions above may seem to be a daunting task, but you may be surprised how quickly a program design emerges once you sit down to work on it. You may be instinctively operating with a set of answers but just need to write them down.

8. *You have outcomes for your programs and a way to measure those outcomes.* Funders are looking for results, so don't bother to submit your grant proposal if you haven't spent some time thinking about this: how will the lives of participants be transformed as a result of your work? Make your program outcomes as concrete and specific as possible, and describe, in detail, how you will measure those outcomes. This idea of developing program outcomes is a new one for many people in ministry. Many of us think, "We're doing the work of the Lord, so what other results do we need?" But foundation and corporate funders will want to see more from you than your service to God. For example, if you're helping homeless people, do they find jobs or housing because of the work you are doing? Or if you have an academic program for youth, do your participants start doing better in school? Setting program outcomes is much more than a way to get the attention of funders. It helps an organization become more focused and helps staff and volunteers understand the goals they are working toward. See chapter 8 for more information on how to set program outcomes and measure them.

Weigh Each Funding Opportunity

Once you starting writing grant proposals, you may be tempted to pursue every grant opportunity that presents itself. There are many, and you'll become aware of more and more as you begin to research funders and write proposals. Instead, I'd recommend that you weigh the advantages and disadvantages of each funder and search for ones that fit best with your ministry and its programs. You may find that you spend less time on grant-proposal writing with greater success.

Key Questions

1. What types of fundraising activities (other than grant-proposal writing) could your ministry engage in to build a broad funding base?

   _____

   _____

   _____

   _____

2. What are the advantages of grant funding for your ministry?

   _____

   _____

   _____

   _____

3. What are the disadvantages of grant funding for your ministry?

   _____

   _____

   _____

   _____

4. Is your ministry ready to write grant proposals? How do you know?

   _____

   _____

   _____

   _____

3

Types of Grants and Funders

Before you begin to write your grant proposal, you'll need to look out into the landscape of funding and understand who's out there. As you gain some tools and knowledge, the landscape will begin to make more sense and you'll be able to answer these questions: Who are the funders and what do they like to support? How is each type of funder unique, and how can we approach each type?

This chapter describes the types of funders you will most likely engage with as you prepare and submit your grant proposals: private and community foundations, corporate foundations, and corporate-giving programs. I've also included information on mission funding through churches.

In addition to understanding the types of funders, you'll need to know what type of grant to request. When I first started writing grants and funders asked, "What will you use the money for?" I thought it was a strange question. Of course, we were going to use the money to pay the bills! What funders are really asking is this: are you requesting an unrestricted, general operating grant, or will you designate the funding toward a particular program or capital expense, or to build capacity within your organization? Be clear about which of these four types of grants you are asking for in your proposal, so that the funder doesn't have to guess.

Types of Grants

There are several types of grants you can request when approaching a funder, and these are typically listed in a funder's guidelines.

General operating grant

A general operating grant supports the overall expenses of an organization and is not designated by the donor for any particular program or expense. Your organization gets to decide how to spend the grant money. This is the least restrictive type of grant and can be the most helpful to you, since you can use it wherever funding is most needed. Unfortunately, fewer and fewer foundation and corporate funders make general operating grants, preferring to focus their funding on program or project grants instead.

Program or project grant

The program or project grant is designated for a particular activity and its associated expenses. Program and project grants have become much more popular with funders in recent years, as foundations and corporations have targeted their grants to achieve measurable impact.

Expenses that could be covered by a program grant include program staff salaries and benefits, supplies, equipment, transportation, special events, and other program costs. Usually (depending on the funder's instructions), you can also include a certain percentage of your administrative expenses in a program request. For example, a certain percentage of your liability insurance, postage, phone usage, and printing costs could be put in the expense budget of a particular program.

Chapter 8 details how to prepare your overall grant proposal. Program grant proposals, in particular, need to include:

- *A demonstrated need for your program.*
- *A clear program plan,* detailing goals and objectives for your program, as well as activities and the timeline for carrying them out. Show the funder that you've spent the necessary time planning the program and that you have thought it through completely.
- *The "niche" your program fills.* What makes your program different from similar programs? Thinking about what sets you apart will increase your chances of getting funded.

- *A detailed program budget.* You will need to develop a program budget that is detailed enough for the funder to understand how his or her money is to be used. Don't just put in a line item for "equipment," for example. Break it out in more detail, showing expenses for computers or sports equipment, for example.
- *An evaluation plan that clearly demonstrates the impact of the proposed program and how you plan to measure that impact.* Funders make program grants to achieve focused impact, so they'll want to see the results you are achieving in concrete terms.
- *Staff members and volunteers who have the capacity to implement the program.* The funder will want to see that the people who work with you can actually pull off what you are proposing to do.

Capital grant

A capital grant is targeted toward bricks-and-mortar building projects or the purchase of major equipment. Your group could use a capital grant to purchase a building, renovate an existing space, replace the computers in a computer lab, or purchase a vehicle, for example. Funders who make capital grants will usually indicate specifically how they would like their money to be spent.

Typically, funders like to have an existing relationship with your organization before they consider a capital grant, though there are some exceptions. An ideal scenario would begin with a funder supporting the start-up and growth of your youth development program. Now the program has grown to the point that you need to purchase your own building. You present a proposal to a funder that already supports your group, requesting funding for the purchase of the building, as well as some of the needed renovations.

One tip about capital grants: I often meet people in ministry who want to purchase a building, and then start a program. Some folk see owning a building as a way to bring to their organization the credibility it lacks. Also, by owning your own building, you can avoid the hassles and humility involved in leasing from someone else and having to share space. In my experience, however, groups that strengthen their organizational capacity and develop their programs *before* they secure a building are more successful in just about every regard. Once you've done this work of strengthening what you started with, you will be better prepared for building purchase and ownership.

1. You will have a better sense of the type and amount of space you need.
2. You will have more and longer-term relationships with funders who would be willing to make capital grants.
3. You will have more of a funding base to pay for the increased expenses of owning a building.
4. You will likely have a larger staff that can assist with the process of planning and implementing capital fundraising and managing a building.

Capital grant proposals, in particular, need to document:

1. *The need for the capital project.* For example: "We have to turn 20 people away from our clinic every week because we don't have enough space to serve them." Or the project may be needed to maximize efficiency—moving all programs and staff to the same location or purchasing a vehicle to reduce staff time spent on transportation, for example.
2. *The impact that the capital project will have on your organization and its programs.* Examples:

   • We anticipate being able to serve 30 percent more families.
   • We will be able to add a program for senior citizens in our community.
   • The after-school tutoring program will be more effective when students have a quiet place to study.

3. *A detailed budget for the building project* to be undertaken or the equipment to be purchased.

4. *Information on the property to be purchased and designs for the renovations or new building* (if you are requesting money for a building project). Funders will probably want to see that key professionals have been involved in helping you choose your new place and develop a plan and budget for it—building inspectors, architects, and general contractors, for example.

5. *Information on how the building or equipment will be maintained* after the term of the capital grant has expired. Owning a building will add many expenses to your budget, including maintenance and utilities. Funders will want to see a plan showing that you can afford to sustain the building or equipment over the long term.

Capacity-building grant

A capacity-building grant supports special projects designed to help you move forward organizationally in some significant ways. Examples of capacity building efforts include:

- Hiring a consultant who leads your organization through a strategic planning process.
- A feasibility study looking at the relocation of your group to a larger facility.
- Training and consulting to develop program evaluation processes.

Your current funders may be the best prospects for a capacity-building grant. Because they are already invested in your organization, these funders might be willing to give you an "extra" grant for capacity-building for a year or two. When I worked for an urban ministry organization, one large funder that supported our programs for families and children gave us an additional grant one year to fund a strategic-planning process and to hire an evaluation consultant. The money proved to be a good investment, enabling the organization to clarify its focus and its future.

Types of Funders

In addition to understanding the types of grants, you'll need to know about the types of funders before you write your grant proposal.

Corporate funders

Many corporations make grants or in-kind contributions to non-profit organizations in the community, frequently focusing their funding on the geographic area where the corporation is based and on nonprofits that involve employees from the company. While many corporate leaders are sincere in their desire to see their community flourish, improving the image of the corporation is typically one of the motives for corporate giving. Corporate grants help create a positive impression of the company among consumers, who may feel better about buying from a company that is a "good corporate citizen." For example, you may notice signs when you are shopping at certain businesses indicating that the company gives "5 percent of pre-tax profits to charity." Corporate giving can also generate more publicity for the company's brands, particularly if philanthropy is tied to the company's core businesses.

Larger corporations may have both a foundation and a corporate-giving program. Check to see if a corporation has both, then research each to see where your organization fits best. In some cases, it may be possible for you to submit proposals to both the company's foundation and its giving program, depending on the policies of the corporation.

Corporate foundations

Some corporations form their own foundations, primarily to institutionalize the giving function and to gain a tax advantage. Forming a foundation demonstrates that the corporation takes its philanthropy seriously and intends to give back to the community over the long term. Starting a foundation can also help the company maintain its giving even when the economy declines, providing an opportunity to create an endowment or other financial reserves that can sustain grant-making when revenues are down.

In my experience, corporate foundations have more formal guidelines and procedures than corporate-giving programs (described below). Foundations usually develop written materials and a Web site that provides detailed information to grant seekers. Also, corporate foundations typically have staff members whose job is to relate to grantees and to review requests, so you will probably find it easier to reach a real person who can answer your questions. Staff members at corporate foundations often play a role similar to that of a program officer at a private foundation, a position described later in this chapter.

Corporate-giving programs

Some companies have corporate-giving programs that distribute funds, separate from the foundation at the corporation. These programs are often administered through the marketing or community-relations department of a corporation. Typically, companies provide less written information on these giving programs than on corporate foundations. If there are written guidelines, they may be less specific, and you may find that there is no published annual report or list of grantees (though I have seen exceptions). You may need to be more creative in researching and finding this type of funder.

I've often found out about corporate-giving programs by networking with other nonprofit executives (discussing who's funding what) or by keeping a close eye on the business section of the newspaper. Since one of the purposes of corporate giving is to generate positive publicity for the company, it's not unusual to read in the newspaper about major corporate gifts made to local nonprofit groups.

Another tip: some corporate-giving programs provide donations through individual branch offices or stores. Retail stores often use this approach, making larger grants through their corporate offices and smaller gifts through their stores. Gifts through the stores are often decided on by the store manager or a committee of employees from that location.

Other types of corporate gifts

Many corporations extend their philanthropy far beyond typical grant-making activities. You may be able to secure additional resources for your organization through in-kind gifts, corporate sponsorships, and matching gifts.

1. *In-kind gifts.* Most larger corporations also make in-kind gifts, distributing products or providing services for free or at a much-reduced cost. Though grant-making gets more attention, in-kind gifts can be the same as cash for your organization if you are able to receive supplies and equipment you need to run your programs. In my nonprofit career, I've received in-kind donations of computers, software, books, food, office furniture, vehicles, printing, legal help, and property.

2. *Employee matching gifts.* Corporations will frequently match employee gifts made to nonprofit organizations. When you send out mailings to current or prospective individual donors, put something on the pledge card that refers to matching gifts—a check box with a statement like "Yes, my employer will match my gift," with a line next to it where the employee can write in the name of the company. You can follow up with donors who check that box.

Corporate sponsorships

Corporate sponsorships, sometimes referred to as "cause-related" marketing, are another strategy used by corporations both to serve the community and to increase the visibility of the corporation and its products and services. Corporations may consider underwriting the cost of a major event that involves your organization, such as a theater premiere, a conference on an issue of concern to your community, or your fundraising gala. Some corporations also raise money for nonprofits by tying their giving to the purchase or use of certain brands. For example, General Mills sponsors the "Save Lids to Save Lives" campaign through its Yoplait yogurt brand. The brand has contributed $15.5 million to breast cancer–related causes based on the number of yogurt lids sent to the company by consumers.

Typically, the marketing departments of corporations handle the sponsorships and cause-related marketing projects, so you will probably be talking to different people at the company from those you spoke with when you applied for a grant. Sometimes it's possible to get a sponsorship *and* a grant, so don't assume you can ask for only one.

Characteristics of Corporate Funders

Corporations vary widely in the way they practice philanthropy, but in my experience, it's possible to make a few generalizations about corporate funders as a group.

Strong ties to geography

Most corporate funders give in the geographic areas where they have a strong presence; that is, where employees live and where the company's offices, stores, and plants are located. They are unlikely to give in geographic areas where the company does not have a presence.

It used to be that major corporations gave funding almost exclusively in the geographic area where the company's headquarters was located. However, this is beginning to change, and many corporate funders now make contributions also where branches, factories, and stores are located across the region or the country.

Employee involvement

Corporate funders also consider whether one or more of their employees are involved with the organization seeking a grant. In fact, a number of corporate funders have made this connection a requirement for grant seekers. What's the reason? Corporations look at employee involvement as a kind of endorsement of nonprofit organizations, helping corporate leaders to choose among many worthy organizations in the communities where they give. This tie between volunteerism and grant-making also helps encourage employees to get involved in the community by rewarding the time they invest with a grant for the organization they serve.

If your group plans to seek corporate dollars, make yourself aware of the corporate affiliations of your board members, staff, and other volunteers. Having an employee of the corporation send a letter or e-mail on your behalf may make all the difference as your grant proposal is being considered. Your volunteers who have high-level jobs in the corporation may have more of a voice in funding decisions, but even employees who work at support jobs or on the factory floor could help turn a grant decision your way. So don't look only for corporate vice-presidents or CEOs to volunteer for your group and to speak on your behalf.

Finding ways to engage corporate volunteers is one way to build funding relationships with the corporations in your community. Some companies even have volunteer coordinators who can help you find people in the company who would be interested in volunteering with your group. These volunteer programs can be a source of board members, program volunteers, and administrative help. You may be able to get a group of corporate volunteers to help with special programs or events at your organization.

Concerns about giving to faith-based efforts

Corporate funders tend to be more nervous about donating to faith-based groups, mainly because corporations have more stakeholders than other types of funders. Corporations have a number of constituencies that follow and care about what causes the company supports—employees, senior management, the board of directors, customers, and stockholders. Giving to faith-based groups may anger or alienate stakeholders who subscribe to a different religion or who practice no religion at all. That said, I have been successful over the years at attracting funding for faith-based programs from corporate donors, but the funding was always for programs that had no faith content at all, and the corporate staff needed reassurance on that point before the company would make a grant.

Ties to the core goals of the corporation

Another trend in corporate giving is making grants that are directly related to the core goals of the corporation. For example, you might find a food company that makes grants in the area of nutrition, or a newspaper company that funds writing and journalism programs. You might even find particular brands of the company tied to specific initiatives—the "Spiffy Peanut Butter" nutrition challenge for kids, for example.

Alex Cirillo, vice president of the 3M Foundation, notes, "Companies are more aware of the alignment of giving with corporate reputation and corporate goals. These connections have become stronger for corporations because of public opinion, greater regulation, and the demands of shareholders in the interests of company citizenship"[1] Because 3M is a corporation that depends on a well-educated workforce with skills in science, technology, engineering, and math, the 3M Foundation now targets 50 percent of its giving to educational initiatives that encourage children to go into these disciplines.

Community Foundations

Community foundations may be a potential source of funding for your group as well. They both raise and distribute funding, typically in a particular geographic area or in relation to a particular issue.

Many cities around the country have community foundations that focus their work in that city, raising money from the community, researching issues and directing their resources toward those issues. Where I live, for example, the local community foundations have helped focus attention on issues of child poverty and school readiness by researching issues and making targeted investments. Community foundations aren't always geographically based. Sometimes they focus on a particular demographic group, such as women or African Americans; at other times they might form around a particular issue, such as early childhood education.

Community foundations typically provide contributions through several funding streams. Usually there is an overall competitive grant-making process through the foundation, with specific guidelines, deadlines, and review processes. If you look closer at a community foundation's Web site or written materials, you may see also that there are other foundations set up within the foundation, with their own review processes. Keep in mind that these separate foundations may have deadlines and areas of interest different from those of the community foundation itself.

Another possible source of funding through a community foundation is donor-advised funds. These are funds started by individuals or families in the community who want to make contributions to charitable organizations. Many community foundations have hundreds or even thousands of these funds. You can usually find them listed on the foundation's Web site or in the annual report. Many community foundations make a large percentage of their donations through donor-advised funds.

Donors to the donor-advised funds pay a fee to the community foundation to manage their investments, and then the donors advise the foundation every year as to where they would like their contributions to go. In my experience, you are most likely to get funding from a donor-advised fund if you know the individual or family that has set it up. But some community foundations have foundation staff work to match organizations with these donors. Check out the community foundation's Web site to see if there is an application form you can submit for this process.

Many community foundations see their role as extending far beyond grant-making. It's not unusual to see community foundations play a convening role, drawing together people and organizations to discuss and address key issues. Community foundations I'm aware of have held conferences recently on black philanthropy and the capacity of faith-based organizations. Some community foundations also engage in research, devoting resources to documenting issues and problems, developing new strategies, and identifying other models around the country. If your ministry is working on the cutting edge of an issue that has not been well-documented, you might consider connecting with your local community foundation to see if it will research the issue.

In my experience, the following statements are true about community foundations:

1. *Community foundations are more responsive to community trends and research than other types of funders.* Part of the job of the community foundation is to keep track of the heartbeat of the community—who's coming, who's going, who's succeeding, and who is suffering. Monitoring that heartbeat produces information that influences grant-making in a direct and often rapid way.

2. *Community foundations may be more willing to tackle controversial issues than private or corporate foundations.* Corporations have an image to maintain, and that can work to keep them away from controversy. Sometimes this is the case with private foundations too.

3. *Community foundations have a strong preference for collaboration, particularly broad-based community collaborations.* I've stressed throughout the book that most funders prefer to fund collaborative efforts, but this is especially true of community foundations. You might find community foundations convening and then funding community collaborations that involve people from a variety of organizations within the public, corporate, and nonprofit sectors.

4. *Community foundations are often more interested in supporting capacity-building than other types of funders.* It's not unusual to see funds or even foundations within a community foundation dedicated to helping nonprofit organizations in the area move forward by providing funds for training, evaluation, strategic planning, and other capacity-building activities.

5. *Community foundations are often more interested in supporting grassroots organizations and issues affecting people of color than other types of funders.* If your ministry is run by or serves people of color, you might take a look at your local community foundation to see what types of groups they have supported in the past. Some community foundations have started "minority endowment funds" that raise money

from people of color and then give it to issues affecting those minority groups.

Private Foundations

The giving practices of private foundations vary so widely that it is difficult to make generalizations about this type of funder. The way private foundations operate is heavily influenced by the size of their assets, whether they are family foundations, and whether there is a paid staff helping to influence and direct funding decisions.

Many private foundations are family foundations—or at least they began that way. The Donors Forum of Chicago estimates that two-thirds of the estimated 44,000 private foundations in the U.S. are family-managed. The number of family foundations nationwide has increased significantly in the past several years; you will likely be talking with this type of funder as you search for grant opportunities. The Council on Foundations defines a family foundation as "an independent private foundation whose funds are derived from members of a single family. At least one family member must continue to serve as an officer or board member of the foundation, and as the donor, they or their relatives play a significant role in governing and/or managing the foundation throughout its life."[2]

The giving priorities of a family foundation are likely to be heavily influenced by the interests of family members. For example, family members might direct grants to colleges or universities they attended or to geographic areas where the family has lived. You can usually spot a family foundation by its name, or by a list of trustees that includes several people with the same last name. It's revealing to track how family interests influence foundation priorities. Read through the list of a family foundation's grantees, and you may see patterns in giving based on what Grandma was interested in, what the grandson struggled with, and what Mom did in her 20s. I'm aware of a corporate leader who, with his wife, formed a family foundation that focuses on integrative medicine—healing approaches that treat the whole person: mind, body, and spirit. This focus was a good fit for the family because the man's wife had been diagnosed with cancer several years earlier, and she found great help and comfort in combining Western medical treatment with alternative approaches such as acupuncture and meditation.

Statistically, family foundations are more likely than other types of funders to give to religious organizations. If the family that runs the foundation is oriented toward spiritual matters at all, your ministry may be more successful seeking grants here, for example, than if you applied to a corporation for funding for the same program. Family foundations also tend to be more entrepreneurial, investigating new kinds of projects and issues to support. Statistically, they give out less money than other types of funders. The Foundation Center reported that in 2004 over half of family foundations nationwide reported giving less than $50,000 total in one year.

Another characteristic to note about family foundations: many of them are turning the reins over to the next generation in the family. So if you submit a request to a family foundation, don't be surprised if you find yourself dealing with someone under age 35. Chairing the board of the largest family foundation in Minnesota, for example, is a woman in her early 30s, the granddaughter of the foundation's founders. In my experience, members of this next generation tend to be much more results-oriented and like to fund grassroots efforts. They are less likely than their predecessors to focus giving on the larger "prestige" nonprofits in a community and may instead be willing to fund smaller, community-based efforts.

Private foundations can vary greatly in size, from funders that give out just a few thousand dollars a year to those that give out millions of dollars annually and have hundreds of staff members. In general, private foundations with fewer assets tend to be run by family members or other members of the foundation's board of trustees. In this case, having a personal connection to a family member or board member may get your grant proposal a better hearing. If you don't have that personal connection, it can be difficult to get someone on the phone to obtain more information or to arrange a meeting, since there may be no paid staff members or formal office. Also, the process for seeking a grant can be much less formal than for larger foundations. Small foundations will probably require you to submit a written grant proposal, but they may ask for fewer reports and attachments and for a proposal of fewer pages (though I have seen exceptions).

Some smaller foundations have a policy of "no unsolicited requests." If you see that phrase written in their materials or in a foundation index, it means that the funder has a set list of organizations it supports and is not interested in receiving requests from groups it doesn't already have a relationship with. Unless you hear otherwise from a staff or board member, I would advise that you not bother submitting a proposal to a foundation with a policy of "no unsolicited requests," since it will probably be a waste of your time.

Staffing at private foundations

Some private foundations are large enough to hire staff members to administer and oversee the grant-making process. Program officers are common in many larger private foundations. Their duties can vary, but generally, a program officer is responsible for:

1. *Helping to shape the giving priorities of the foundation in a particular area.* Many program officers will specialize in one or several areas of interest for a foundation, such as youth development, health, religion, or the environment. It is common for program officers to have worked in organizations in their area of specialty.
2. *Communicating those priorities to the public.*
3. *Working one-on-one with grant seekers.* Once you've read the foundation's guidelines, you may need to call the program officer to get clarification or advice on submitting your proposal.
4. *Reviewing grant proposals.*
5. *Making site visits.* You may get to meet the program officer face-to-face when he or she pays a visit to gather more information about your organization and to get a sense of your work.
6. *Making recommendations to the foundation board about which proposals should be funded.*

The amount of influence a program officer has varies with the organization. Some foundations have established a culture in which the program officers make recommendations and the board of the foundation almost always supports them. In this situation, the program officer has a great deal of power to decide where funding goes. In other private foundations, program officers play more of an administrative and public-relations role. They handle details, answer questions, and are the "face" of the foundation in a community. They may prepare summaries of the proposals for the foundation board, but the board makes the decisions about which organizations are funded.

Church Giving Programs

Though this book is focused on foundation and corporate funders, I include information on funding from churches as well, since these could be a fruitful source from which to seek contributions for your ministry. If you've been working in ministry for a while, you know that congregations vary widely in their theologies, structures, processes, and cultures. As a result, there is also a great variety within church giving programs. Some are more structured, others informal. Some seek strong input from the pastor; others let laypeople make decisions. If you are serious about building funding relationships with churches, you'll need to be willing to study each congregation carefully before approaching it.

Church giving programs don't usually provide the same type of information to grant seekers as foundations and corporations do. I've seen very few churches, for example, that publish a list of grantees. Some churches have a written application and a set of guidelines; others do not. The information you receive about church funding may have to come from relationships you build with church staff and members, and as I note below, these relationships will strongly influence your chance of being funded by the church anyway.

Though church giving practices vary widely, I believe the following generalizations can be made:

1. *Money follows relationships.* Church funding has become more and more like corporate funding, in that many churches now require that their members be involved in an organization before a financial gift is made. "It's not just about the money; it's about the relationships," the pastor of one church said to me recently, and I hear that again and again as I talk with pastors and church leaders. Churches want their members to be "doing good" in the community, and you can help them to do that. If you start your relationship by providing volunteer opportunities for church members, you will soon have a group of enthusiastic boosters for your funding request to the church.

   For example, if your ministry builds affordable housing in an urban neighborhood, you may be able to partner with churches in the area to provide volunteers. Getting volunteers to come into the neighborhood to help with the building will spur awareness of needs in the city as well as excitement about the work you are doing. For volunteers, seeing a situation with their own eyes and using their own hands to help can be a powerful experience, and it is much more engaging than reading a newsletter or listening to a speech. Once you have church volunteers involved in your organization, you can ask them to advocate on your behalf with their congregations. They can bring you information on funding processes and put in a good word for you as your request is considered.

   One tip before you invite church volunteers into your organization: be sure you have work for them to do that is meaningful both for the volunteers and for your organization. Avoid situations in which volunteers have little to do or are contributing so little that it isn't worth the time and effort you spend organizing them. Also, volunteers may need training before they participate in your program. Training could be provided on such topics as program policies, strategies for working with participants, and diversity training that equips volunteers to work with participants of an ethnic or socioeconomic group different from their own.

2. *Application processes vary.* Churches vary widely in their application processes. Over the years, some of the most detailed grant requests I have submitted have been to churches, with application forms that seem to request information about everything, including the applicant's theological beliefs on various issues. Other church application processes are much less formal. You may simply be asked to send in a couple of pages describing your ministry. Some congregations accept proposals on an ongoing basis; others have specific deadlines.

3. *A committee makes the decisions.* Often it's not just up to the pastor or staff of a church to direct funding decisions. Usually a committee of laypeople from the church has that responsibility, often the mission committee or outreach committee. Larger churches may have several committees involved in making the funding decisions—some focused on international missions, others focused on urban missions. This distinction is important for you to know so that you can direct your request to the right people and understand the process for reviewing your proposal. The best way to approach is to ask a volunteer from the church to connect you with the right committee.

   As part of a church funding request, you may be asked to make a presentation about your ministry to the committee that reviews proposals. Be sure to ask about the preferred length of the presentation, as other organizations may be presenting on the same night, and you won't want to infringe on other people's time. I've found that church people like to hear stories about the ministry and enjoy viewing photographs or videos. Give them a sense of the people that your ministry is helping and the impact that is being made, and you'll increase your chances of being funded.

4. *Denominational ties can make a difference.* If your ministry group has a denominational tie, you may have more success going to the local churches of that denomination to seek funding. Often, organizations in the same denomination see each other as "family," and that perception may get you

more of a hearing than you'd get from churches outside your denomination. You should also pay attention to funding that may be available through your denominational offices at the national level. Sometimes special funds are set aside within a denomination to help with start-up ministries or programs that focus on a particular population, such as women, immigrants, or the elderly.

You may want to start with churches in your denomination, but don't ignore those in other denominations. I've seen plenty of funding given across denominational lines, and I am now working in a community that has seen a recent trend of cross-denominational church partnerships.

5. *Developing a deeper partnership with a church can lead to longer and larger funding commitments.* Rather than just paying attention to your church donors once a year when you ask them for money, you may want to pursue more of a full-fledged church partnership with at least some of the congregations that give to you. Developing church partnerships is hard work, but such linkages have many benefits, not least the potential for increasing the size of the financial gifts made to your ministry. When you form deeper relationships with the staff and parishioners of a congregation through the partnership, you may find ways to collaborate and to share ideas, facilities, and supplies. You may also find that your own congregation and your partner churches grow spiritually in new ways. Coming together around an issue, particularly across denominational lines, can be a transforming experience for everyone involved.

Your church partners may also allow you to speak to their congregations about your ministry, providing a deeper connection between the church members and your ministry. Pursue these speaking opportunities, and always say yes when they are offered. Speaking about your ministry face-to-face can help encourage people in your partner church to volunteer with your ministry, pray for you, get their friends involved, and make financial donations as individuals.

Which Funding and Funders Are Best for You?

When I began fundraising, I wondered how I would ever learn to identify the best types of funders for my current project. With all the various funding options, where should we focus? The answer does become clearer over time. As I recommend in chapter 6, you'll need to study the funders, examining their priorities, areas of focus, and grant requirements, to determine which ones best fit your program or organization. And then you'll just have to try a few. You may find that corporations seem to love your job-training program, but that it's much harder to get church donors engaged with that project. Or family foundations might be the right fit for your "arts for everyone" program, and corporations might not be interested in it at all. Whom to send proposals to becomes clearer over time, as you develop relationships in the funding community and begin to understand how the different types of funders operate.

Key Questions

1. What types of grants are you seeking for your ministry— general operating, program, capital, or capacity-building?

   _____

   _____

   _____

   _____

2. In your local funding community, which types of funders would be the best fit for your ministry? Why?

   a. Corporate foundations or corporate giving programs
   b. Private foundations
   c. Community foundations
   d. Church missions programs

   _____

   _____

   _____

   _____

4

What Do Funders Really Want?

Grant-making is a competitive business, and most funding institutions approve just a fraction of the funding requests they receive. Organizations that successfully secure grants are constantly working to think like funders—imagining what it is like to sift through proposals, to talk to people seeking funds, and finally, to make decisions about where to give money. So put yourself in the funder's shoes: imagine that you are a staff member at a local foundation that receives from 20 to 100 grant proposals a week. The number of proposals coming into the foundation is overwhelming, and most of them present organizations that meet a real need in the community. What makes one proposal stand out from the rest of the pile on your desk? From my experience and from what foundation and corporate staff have told me, these are the key issues that are considered in reviewing grant proposals, listed in no particular order.

Your proposal matches the funder's values

Study the funder, and tailor your proposal to each one's values; otherwise, don't bother sending the proposal at all. This may be the single most important piece of advice offered in this book. Every proposal you send out should be different (perhaps just slightly), responding to the interests and values of the funder. Of course, you should always guard against compromising the mission of your organization as you tailor your proposal to a funder. For example, don't change the focus of your mission from North Minneapolis to South Minneapolis just to get the money.

How will you learn about the values of a funder? Read everything funders put out about themselves—written guidelines and annual reports as well as Web sites. The material funders generate about themselves will typically tell you these things:

- their areas of interest.
- the geographic area on which they are focused.
- the average size of a grant made to a group like yours.
- what they do *not* fund.
- what they want included in a proposal.

Look through the list of nonprofit groups that the funder has supported, and you may learn something about funding patterns that does not appear in the guidelines. For example, funders may not directly state that they prefer to support faith-based organizations, and yet you may see many faith-based groups in the list of grantees.

You have financial support from their peers

It seems unfair, but money follows money. The first $5,000 grant you get for your program will do a lot more than fund $5,000 worth of programming. It will also indicate to other foundations and corporations that your program is worth considering, that it may very well be a fundable project in the eyes of the philanthropic community. That is why funders will almost always ask for a list of other funders that support your group. Funders want to see if any of their colleagues have given you the stamp of approval.

As I mentioned in chapter 2, some foundations and corporations serve as "gatekeepers" in the funding community, and their stamp of approval will help you to secure funding from other foundations. Often these "gatekeepers" are among the largest funding organizations in the area or are known for a rigorous review process. Getting a grant from one of these gatekeepers communicates to the rest of the funding community that your group is worthy of support and that other foundations might want to take a look at you as well.

You have measurable outcomes for your programs

In interviews for this book, this issue rose to the top for almost every foundation staff member. Foundation and corporate staff are tired of being hit over the head with needs; most of them are well aware of the needs in the community. What they are hungry for are programs and organizations that achieve concrete results in addressing those needs.

Being able to demonstrate those concrete results will require your ministry to establish measurable program outcomes that answer this question: "What will change in the lives of your participants because of your work?" For example, if you are proposing to start a transitional housing program for unemployed women in your area, don't just describe the need and the number of people you intend to serve. Focus on what will change for the women through the program:

- The women will secure living-wage employment.
- The women and their families will achieve greater stability in housing.
- The children in these families will improve their performance in school.

You'll also need to identify how you will measure your outcomes. You might survey participants or volunteers, conduct focus groups, or establish quantitative goals that you will measure against. However you develop your outcomes and measuring tools, just be sure that you have a strong possibility of delivering on them. It's easy to set lofty goals, more difficult to implement the program that will help you achieve them.

If this outcome-focused thinking is new to you, you might consider participating in some training that will help you develop the skills you need to evaluate your programs. The United Way in your area may sponsor such training. Nonprofit management-training programs at local colleges and universities would also be a good place to check.

Hiring an evaluation consultant is another way to bring this capacity to your organization. An experienced evaluator can lead you through a process with key staff members and volunteers, helping you agree on outcomes and begin to implement an evaluation program.

You collaborate with other organizations in your area

Gone are the days when nonprofits could get funding for a "one-agency-only" approach to a community issue. Funders now focus their giving on collaborative approaches that draw together a diversity of expertise and strengths. You will likely be asked to include with your proposal a list of collaborative partners, identifying how you work with each partner. This focus on collaboration helps both nonprofits and funders in several ways:

- It encourages nonprofits to get into the community they serve and to form relationships, a key to success in just about any type of nonprofit work.
- It helps reduce duplication, as nonprofits have been forced to justify why they aren't partnering with groups that are doing something similar.
- It draws together a diverse and complex group of organizations to address diverse and complex issues in the community.

As you form collaborations, look for groups that share your values and goals, whose leaders can form positive working relationships with each other. Keep in mind that collaboration takes more time than going it alone, so be prepared to put together collaborations well in advance of funding deadlines, rather than trying to slap together a group of partners at the last minute.

You have grassroots involvement and community support

Do you have strong and positive relationships with the communities that are the focus of your work? Funders look to make sure that you are not just "doing to" your participants, but "serving with" them. For example, if you are developing a community arts program for teenagers, have you involved artists, arts organizations, and teens in the process of planning and implementing your program?

Inviting people from the communities you serve into the program planning process will lead to a much more successful program and will also increase your chances of getting funded. Involve potential program participants, but also other organizations and individuals that have extensive knowledge of the community.

Invite community representatives into the planning process *before* you've made up your mind specifically about what you are going to do, rather than pulling them in at the last minute to endorse something you have already developed. Inviting people to the party at the last minute can be offensive to them and make it harder to involve them once the program is up and running. You'll also miss out on some great input at critical points in the development of your program, and the program may be less successful as a result.

Some corporations and foundations also look for community involvement on the boards of organizations they support. If your nonprofit serves a particular geographic community, for example, you might consider having residents of that community serving on your board. Inviting one or two of the people being served by your programs is another way to accomplish this aim. An employment program might involve a participant in the job-training program and a local employer, for example. This approach makes sense. Boards will want to listen to the experienced and competent voices that speak on behalf of the communities being served.

You have demonstrated success

Funders also like organizations that have demonstrated the capacity to run successful programs and to manage themselves effectively. This proven success helps to reduce the risk that a grant will be wasted on programming that never quite gets off the ground. Demonstrating your successes to a funder doesn't mean that your organization has to be large and old; you just need to show the funder that you are moving forward with one or two of the initiatives you've been dreaming about.

In particular, foundation and corporate staff like to see program initiatives that have set clear outcomes and have achieved at least some of them. Even if your programs are relatively small, be sure to tell about what you've achieved so far. Funders will also be looking for positive signs that your organization is moving forward—for example, a growing group of volunteers or the development of a strategic plan. Don't be afraid to boast of your successes, and be sure to highlight progress, even if you feel like you've made only small steps.

If you are a new organization, the funders' focus on demonstrated success can make it difficult to secure your first grants. Here are a few strategies to try if you're new:

1. *Try a short-term pilot of your project and measure its impact.* There is no substitute for presenting concrete program results to funders. Launching a pilot of your program and evaluating it is one way to get preliminary but concrete program results that will help attract additional dollars.

    Sometimes raising money for a pilot is easier, because you are typically looking for a smaller amount of money and a shorter-term commitment from funders, making it a lower-risk investment for them. When I was helping found a nonprofit management-training program for faith leaders in our community, I approached one funder who had known me for years. After three or four meetings he finally said: "This hasn't been tried, so how do I know it will be successful? It's just an idea at this point." He was right, and what we agreed to was a pilot of the training program. Paying for the pilot was cheap compared to funding the program for the whole year, and we got concrete results that enabled us to approach many other funders successfully.

2. *Emphasize your own previous experience and that of your staff and volunteers.* Your organization may be new, but the people in your organization probably aren't. Be sure to tell the funder about all the experiences your board, staff members, and key volunteers have had that are transferable to this new work, including relevant education, employment, and volunteer experiences.

    I recently helped start a church-based community-development corporation in one of the most disenfranchised and politically divided communities in our state. New efforts were routinely met with suspicion in the community, and some of the funders seemed to share that skepticism. The fact that I had almost 20 years of experience in the nonprofit sector, mostly working in urban neighborhoods, helped us build relationships with the community and with funders. The pastor of the church, another staff member, and several board members also brought strong backgrounds to this new work. Our collective experience helped assure funders that we had a strong chance of succeeding.

3. *Connect or collaborate with a known organization that brings expertise.* Collaborating with a group that already has a positive reputation in the community will also help your chances of securing a grant if you are a new organization. Look for a nonprofit that has been around for a while and has a track record of achieving program results and a positive reputation with funders.

4. *Show that the same program has been tried elsewhere successfully.* Using a model or method that has been studied elsewhere and proven successful can also help bolster your grant request. Even better, look for an existing curriculum or program manual that can be used in your context. Summarize research data on the models or methods in your grant proposal, and then demonstrate the similarities between places where the program was tried and the situation in your community.

You are innovative in your approach

Foundation and corporate funders love to make grants to innovative programs and approaches. In fact, sometimes I think that funders like innovation a little too much, shifting their focus from tried-and-true approaches that could have achieved greater results if they had been funded over a longer period of time. Be sure to highlight the innovative features of your ministry in your proposal. As you take a step back and look at your work, you may find that it is innovative in some of the following ways:

- You are targeting a new population.
- You are using a new program approach.

- You have developed a new kind of collaboration.
- You are working in a geographic area where few other groups are working.
- You are creating results or teaching tools that can help other groups be innovative.

You have a volunteer who is an employee of a corporate funder

Most corporate funders now require that one or more of their employees be involved with a nonprofit before they consider making a grant to the organization. Employee involvement doesn't guarantee that you will get a grant, but it is a prerequisite for being seriously considered in most cases.

To maximize these corporate connections, be sure to find out where your board members and other volunteers are employed. Even if your volunteers aren't in high-level positions in a company, they can still help advocate for your proposal. Include the name of the employee in the text of your grant proposal, then ask the employee to send an e-mail or letter to the funder expressing support for your proposal.

When you are recruiting volunteers or board members, you might want to consider employees of certain companies in your list of candidates to improve your chances of securing a grant from that company. Some large corporations even have a volunteer mobilization office that can help you identify company employees who would be interested in volunteering with your group and bring the skills you need.

Red Flags for Funders

Just as there are positive signs in a proposal that funders search for, there are red flags that you want to avoid waving. These signals will give corporate and foundation staff an unfavorable impression of your organization and may prevent you from getting a grant.

Poor financial records or financial difficulties

You will be asked to send in financial reports, possibly an audit, and both program and organizational budgets with your grant proposal. If you can't produce those documents or if the ones you send in are incomplete or inaccurate, that will raise a red flag for the funder. Corporations and foundations want to know that their grant funds will be managed wisely and will go toward the designated activity.

Funders often shy away from groups that are running deficits, and for understandable reasons. Corporations and foundations want their money to be used to make an impact in the community, not to fill a financial hole for an organization. If you are in a deficit position, your best bet is to raise funds from current individual donors who are willing to give toward eliminating your deficit. You can also cut costs within the organization until the deficit is eliminated. Another option is to present funders with information on why the deficit occurred (sometimes deficits are unavoidable) and present a plan for the reduction or elimination of the deficit, preferably over a short period of time.

If your financial records are a mess, your best strategy is to get professional help immediately. Hire an accountant to sort through everything and to set up a professional bookkeeping system for you. Accounting services don't have to cost a lot. Many accountants work on a consulting basis, just a few hours a week or month. I also recommend that you have a financial audit of your ministry completed each year. An audit provides confirmation of your organization's financial totals and checks your financial processes and procedures. Getting a "clean" audit, with no concerns expressed by the auditor, is reassuring to funders who are reluctant to give to groups that are having financial difficulties.

Unfocused plan

An unfocused or unrealistic plan is another common complaint of foundation and corporate staff. When preparing their funding requests, many nonprofits present plans that are clearly a case of "biting off more than they can chew." In an effort to impress the funder, groups overestimate what is possible in the scope of the program, the number of people who could be served, or the impact that can be achieved. I think it's easy to fall into this trap. Somehow we think that corporations and foundations will take us seriously only if we puff ourselves up to look bigger than we are. This simply isn't true.

In fact, the more I've gotten to know funders, the more I've realized that most of them have a pretty good idea of what it takes to launch new initiatives and to grow an organization. Most funding institutions don't mind supporting small initiatives that grow slowly, at a realistic rate; in fact, they probably prefer to do so. So when you propose your after-school program, consider carefully how long it will realistically take to get it off the ground. Have you allowed yourself enough time to locate a site, hire staff, and recruit both volunteers and participants? Also, how many students can you realistically serve in the first year? It may be more realistic to work toward involving 40 or 50 students than 200. In my experience, funders like grant seekers who talk straight to them about what's possible.

In your proposal, one place you'll demonstrate whether your plan is realistic is in the program-plan section. Most funders will ask you to outline key activities, steps to implementing them, and the timeline for implementation. Omitting several steps in the program-plan section will give the funder a negative impression of your group. Be sure to step back, take a good look at your program, and include all the things you'll need to do to make it a reality.

Besides setting unrealistic goals, ministry groups sometimes propose projects that lack focus, appearing to be "all over the map" and never pinpointing what's to be done and for whom. I find that faith-based organizations, in particular, struggle with finding focus, perhaps because we feel called to love everyone, and that's what ends up as the vision for our organizations: "We want to love everyone, everywhere, all the time." Such a vision lacks focus, and it won't get you very far with funders.

If your organization or program lacks focus, take the time to get focused before you submit a grant. It will make the grant-seeking process more worth your while. Spend some time identifying your target audience, as specifically as you can. You'll need to narrow down your "what"—what outcomes do you hope to achieve, and what will you do to get there? You'll also need to describe where you will carry out the program and how it will be done. Some non-profits use an outside consultant to lead staff and board through this planning process. An outside voice can bring objectivity and insight, and encourage a more creative level of conversation.

Unrealistic budgets

The budget is one of the most important parts of your grant proposal, but I've found that many groups devote little time to developing it. I like to put together the budget first, because it forces me to get right to these two questions: "What are we going to do?" and "How much will it cost?" Funders look for realistic budgets, indicating that you've done your research and understand the actual costs of operating both your program and your organization.

Budgets that are too small put you in a position of trying to accomplish something without enough money to pull it off. Many nonprofits are tempted to put together minuscule budgets for projects, thinking that funders prefer modest aims. Somehow we get it into our heads that we might appear too hungry for cash if we ask for the amount that it actually takes to run our programs. What funders want is an accurate picture of what your project costs. If you need three staff members to pull this off, then put them in the budget. If you need supplies, equipment, food, and computers, put those items in as well. A too-small budget indicates to the funder that you don't fully understand what's involved in launching your program or running your organization. As a result, the funder may question your capacity to do what you've outlined in the grant.

Another budget error is developing one that is too large for the project proposed. Funders are wary of groups that appear to be "dumping" organizational costs into a project budget to cover overhead. An example: a housing program budget that includes the salary for the full-time staff person who serves as the receptionist/secretary for the entire organization. A "too-large" budget may also include too many project staff, given the amount of work to be accomplished, or supplies and equipment that seem excessive.

It can be difficult to develop a budget that is "just right." An important part of the process is being honest with yourself. Ask yourself: "Have I accurately reflected the costs of operating this program?" If the answer is no, you probably need to increase the budget. Also ask yourself: "Are there expenses in this budget that don't belong there?" and "Have I padded the budget to include excessive overhead costs?" If the answer to one or both of these questions is yes, then you need to reduce your budget to reflect actual costs more accurately.

Staff members without capacity or experience to deliver

Funders will also read your proposal looking for staff capacity—the skills and expertise needed to implement programs and run the organization. In ministry work in particular, your success is less about the building and the curriculum than about the staff members you attract. The staff members will make the difference between a program that succeeds spectacularly and one that never gets off the ground.

Depending on the kind of work you propose to do, you may need staff members with specialized credentials. For example, chemical-dependency treatment programs need trained and credentialed chemical-dependency counselors running them. You may need trained therapists or social workers, licensed day-care teachers, or financial professionals with particular credentials. Be sure you demonstrate to the funder that you understand what kinds of staff resources you will need to move forward on your project.

Even for staff positions that do not require licenses or credentials, funders will look to see if you have staff members with a proven track record in the field in which you are working. It also helps to have people working for you who have experience in your context. If you are working in a rural county, for example, a person who has worked only in an urban context may not be the best fit.

As part of evaluating your staff capacity, funders may also look to see if you have a staff-development plan in place. Allocating part of your budget each year for staff training will help you make the case to funding sources that you are committed to maintaining a high-quality staff that works on an ongoing basis to improve its skills and remain up-to-date on issues in the relevant field. Youth-development and social-service agencies, for example, may require staff to attend training on best practices in the field and new program approaches. Some of your staff may need development in administrative and management areas as well, such as volunteer management, office procedures, and fundraising.

Legal problems or other scandals

If your nonprofit gets embroiled in a scandal, it's damaging to everyone involved and makes it even more difficult to attract foundation and corporate donors.

The best strategy is to work hard to keep your policies and procedures in order, so that you can avoid a scandal or a well-publicized lawsuit in the first place. Screen your volunteers, so that you keep convicted sex offenders out. Develop and follow your personnel policies, so that you steer clear of using discriminatory practices. You'll need financial controls as well, so that people who handle money are accountable to someone else within the organization.

Some people assume that that the media and the courts take a more "hands-off" approach to faith-based organizations struggling with legal problems or scandals, since we're devoted to doing good and serving others. To my eye, the opposite seems to be true. As believers, we're supposed to be the ones who live above reproach, and when we don't, it's big news. The resulting storm of negative media attention can take years to recover from.

Sometimes scandals occur even when preventive measures have been put into place. If you are in this unhappy situation, there are a few strategies you can use:

- Get sound legal advice as soon as possible.
- Follow your lawyer's advice about how to handle the staff, board members, or volunteers who have been engaged in illegal or unethical activity. Your lawyer may recommend that you put the offenders on leave for a time. If the problem is serious enough, termination may be justified.
- Develop policies and procedures that will prevent the same thing from happening again. You may need to develop or change your financial or personnel policies or the screening process for staff and volunteers.

All of these changes will enable you to say to the community and to your funders: "We admit we had a problem, and we have made changes to prevent this from happening in the future."

Duplication of existing service or lack of collaboration

If you have a "we're going to save the world all by ourselves" attitude, you probably won't have much success seeking grant funding. Funders now focus on collaboration to such a great extent that most proposals won't be funded without it. Absence of collaboration gives the funder the impression that:

- You aren't aware of the other work that is being done in your community.
- You aren't aware of your own limitations as an organization and the need for collaborative partners who can help fill in those gaps.
- You aren't willing to do the hard work of building relationships and working together.

Some funders will even call other groups in the community to find out more about your organization as they review your proposal. Several funders I have worked with will ask at the site visit for names of two or three groups doing similar work in your area. If everyone the funder calls says, "Never heard of them," then the funder will assume (probably correctly) that you are a group that doesn't connect with the community and the other organizations in it.

On the flip side is the funder who insists that you collaborate with a particular organization. I have encountered such a demand several times in my career, and I would encourage you to avoid giving in to it. Collaboration will make your programs and your fundraising efforts more successful, but you, not the funder, need to choose the appropriate partners for your group. Letting the funder dictate who your partners are can get you into situations where the partnership doesn't work. As a result, the organizations involved are damaged, and the people you serve are hurt.

People closest to the organization don't give money

You may be asked as part of the funding process whether your board members support the organization financially. Your answer needs to be a resounding "Yes!" Funders want to see that the people closest to the organization support it. If they won't give, why should anyone else?

Board members should be asked by the board chair to make an annual gift, emphasizing that they should give at a level that is significant for them. For some board members, "a significant level" might be $5,000 or more; for others, it might be $50 or less. I usually tell board members I work with that our organization should be in the top three nonprofits they give to each year, in the amount they give. Maybe their church, the United Way, or their alma mater gets a bigger gift, but the organization on whose board they serve should be right up there too.

It can feel uncomfortable to ask board members to give money, since so many of them give generously of their time. But your organization needs both time and money to move forward, and foundation and corporate funders care a great deal about whether your board is financially invested. Tell prospective board members before they join the board that they will be asked to make a financial contribution, so that the expectation is clear.

Conflicting views prevail in the nonprofit sector as to whether staff members should be required to give to the organization. I think it's a good idea for staff members to give, but I don't think it should be required. I always make a financial gift to any nonprofit organization I am employed by, usually before I start raising funds from other people. I feel more authentic as a fundraiser if I am supporting the group to which I ask others to give.

Fundraising Etiquette

So far in this chapter, I've highlighted how the content of your proposal can excite or annoy the funder. Certainly, what's written on the paper is important. But you should also know that your behavior toward the funder, in meetings and over the phone, leaves an impression as well. Observing appropriate fundraising etiquette is essential if you are to give your proposal the best chance of getting a positive review.

Here are some tips on relating to foundation and corporate staff in the most courteous way possible.

1. *Don't act as though you are entitled to the money.* Grant-making is a competitive process, and not every proposal gets funded. Funders turn down worthy groups every day, simply because there is not enough money to fund all grant requests.

2. *Do your homework, so that you don't waste the funder's time.* Before engaging with foundation or corporate staff people, read everything funders put out about themselves. Foundation staff frequently tell me how annoying it is to get calls from people seeking grants who have clearly not spent time looking at the Web site to learn about grant priorities and the application process.

3. *Get the names right.* Make sure you understand whom you are to send the proposal to; then confirm the spelling of that person's name and title. Seeing incorrect information at the beginning of the proposal will give funders the impression that your organization doesn't pay attention to details.

4. *Respect the funder's decision-making structures.* If the answer is no, don't make an end run around the person you have been talking to and go to other staff members or to the foundation board.

5. *Be honest.* I've seen enough nonprofits "fudge" the truth in their grant requests that I offer this reminder about the importance of honesty. Be as straightforward as you can in your funding requests, avoiding the temptation to hide the challenges or overemphasize the successes of your organization. Don't inflate your numbers, and don't leave out key pieces of information just because they would reflect poorly on your organization. Several funders I interviewed for this book also said they are bothered when faith-based organi-

zations attempt to hide their faith focus, seeking to appear more like a secular organization to increase their chances of getting funded. As people of faith, we should be committed to telling the truth in all aspects of our lives. From a strictly practical viewpoint, most funders have a broad network of contacts in the community and may very well know what's happening within your organization, even if you haven't included it in your grant proposal. Funders will probably know when you are being dishonest and will thus gain an unfavorable impression of both you and your organization.

6. *Don't be sexist.* This caution should also go without saying, but I've heard enough from female staff members of foundations to know that fundraisers need to be reminded about this gaffe too. Women play a major leadership role in philanthropy in the United States, so if you assume that it's the men who always make the decisions, you will be wrong much of the time. One of my friends heads her family's foundation, reviewing all the grant requests herself and making funding decisions on behalf of her family. She repeatedly runs into fundraisers who are willing to talk only with her husband, because they assume that he must be the decision maker.

7. *Don't yell at the funder.* I've seen it happen too many times. If you're mad at the funder for turning down your request, wait until you're not feeling angry to talk with someone at the foundation or other funding source. Or have someone else make the call.

8. *Always say thank you.* If you get a yes, send a personal thank-you letter to the funder, as quickly as you can. It does matter to grant-makers whether they get thanked.

Think like a funder

If you're working hard to form and run your ministry organization, you may not think much about the funder's perspective—what it's like for foundations and corporations to make decisions about which organizations to fund. But it's worth considering what might be attention-grabbing or alarming about the proposals that funders receive. If you think like a funder and let that approach inform your grantwriting, you'll have a much greater chance of getting your proposal funded.

Key Questions

1. What things that funders look for are present in your ministry?

   _____

   _____

   _____

   _____

2. Do you have any "red flags" in your ministry that would concern funders? If so, what will you do about these red flags?

   _____

   _____

   _____

   _____

5

Approaching Secular Funders

"We want to expand our housing ministry, but we're nervous about approaching foundations and corporate funders. We're concerned that they would expect us to remove the faith component of our program."

"I don't understand why so many foundations have trouble with the faith thing. What's the big deal whether we spend the money on praying with people or providing them with job training? It's all the same thing."

"We know there's grant funding out there somewhere for the day-care center at our church. What we do helps so many children that I know we'll have no trouble getting funding."

To help nonprofit staff and boards understand how to approach secular funders is one reason I wanted to write this book. I encounter many ministry groups that operate with inaccurate assumptions about how and why secular funders make grants, particularly to faith-based organizations. The quotations above are based on statements that I hear frequently from people in ministry. Some faith-based groups assume that grant funding for their ministries is out of the question. That isn't necessarily true. Others assume that getting grant funding for their ministry will be no problem at all. That isn't necessarily the case, either.

Informing yourself about how secular funders think will help you decide whether to approach them for funding. Perhaps more important, you'll need to decide what "faith-based" means for your organization.

What Are Secular Funders?

I broadly define "secular funders" as foundations or corporations that are *not* using their funding to achieve religious or spiritual goals. Frequently, these funders will include a sentence like this in their funding guidelines: "We will not fund religious organizations for religious purposes."

Secular funders display varying degrees of receptiveness to faith-based organizations. Funders are human beings who have their own perceptions of churches, faith, and spiritual matters. You'll need to use your intuition to discern how open a particular funder is to partnering with faith-based organizations. I've found that secular funders think about faith-based organizations in several ways.

"Not with my money" funders don't care whether your organization is faith-based and the programs have spiritual content, so long as someone else funds that part of your work. They might say something like: "We're interested in helping you buy the apartment building, so the program can get started, but we won't fund the program itself."

"Just as long as it works" funders don't really care if you are faith-based, as long as you can demonstrate results. They believe that to solve complex societal problems, everyone has to come to the table, including the faith community. They will ask a lot of questions about your outcomes and how you expect to achieve them.

"Don't tell my boss" will be the approach of individuals who work for some funders—staff who believe personally in the value of supporting faith-based groups but have to defend the official policy of the funding organization they work for. You may receive some coaching from such a person, advising you to leave the spiritual component out of your written proposal, or explaining how you can describe or structure your program in ways that will be more palatable to the funder. Take copious notes and then decide whether you can follow the advice without compromising your vision for ministry.

"Just leave this part out" funders may try to talk you into deleting or changing the faith component of your program or organization. They may like your program idea so much that they want to

make it fit the values of their foundation or corporation. Sometimes this part of the conversation is more subtle—"If you could just change this one thing, I think I could get you some money." Conversations like this are one reason it's important for your group to understand how faith-based you are. You may or may not want to make the proposed changes, but it will be hard to know if you don't have a strong sense of where faith fits in your organization.

In your conversations with secular funders, none of these scenarios may come into play, or several may be at work at once. The point is to keep these in mind so that you can notice what is happening in the course of the conversation.

Just How Faith-Based Are You?

Understanding what faith-based means within your own organization is perhaps the best way you can prepare to approach secular funders. There have been many positive outcomes to the increased visibility of faith-based organizations in recent years, including the creation of new opportunities for funding and partnerships. One of the challenges, however, is the overuse of the phrase "faith-based." There appears to be no common definition of the term "faith-based." When I say "faith-based," I mean programs that are connected to congregations but that don't necessarily have evangelistic content or goals. Someone else, however, may assume that "faith-based" means there is always an explicit religious component focused on converting participants. It's a loaded term, and to partner with secular funders, we need to define in specific terms what "faith-based" means in our own organizations.

One way to assess how faith-based you are is to look at the spiritual content of your programs. Below I list some key questions to ask. Another way is to look at how faith plays a role in the organizational aspects of your ministry such as funding, mission, and the selection of board members. Thinking through these issues will help prepare you to have conversations with secular funders. In the course of such conversations, you could expect to be asked these kinds of questions:

- What are the spiritual components of your program? Prayer, Bible study, discipleship activities, church attendance?
- Is the spiritual component of your program optional or required for participants?
- Is the spiritual component of your program critical to its success?
- Are participants expected to participate in a particular church congregation to be a part of the program?
- Are staff members, board members, and volunteers expected to share the same faith commitment?

Sorting through the answers to these questions isn't always easy. For many of us, faith has become so key to the work we do and so much a part of the way we live that it is difficult to separate it out from all the "other stuff." It seems artificial to make the separation at all. This is difficult work, but I encourage you at least to try to think about the spiritual component as separate before you approach a secular funder. Using the typology of faith-based organizations in the next section will help you think through the spiritual aspect of your ministry.

A Continuum of Faith-Based Organizations

The Working Group on Human Needs and Faith-Based and Community Initiatives is a project of Search for Common Ground, an organization working to transform the way people deal with conflict. The working group put together a report of 29 recommendations "to increase the capacity and effectiveness of community and faith-based organizations in meeting human needs."[1] (To read the full report, go to www.sfcg.org, and search for "29 recommendations.") The report includes a "typology of faith characteristics of social service and educational organizations" that identifies the characteristics of five types of faith-based organizations. I've provided summaries of the types of organizations below (from pages 32–37 of the report), and you'll find a complete description of them in appendix 2. Note that the spiritual content of programs as well as organizational characteristics such as selection of staff are mentioned in each description.

1. In *"faith-saturated" organizations,* "religious faith is very important at all levels, and most staff share the organization's faith commitments. 'Faith-saturated' programs involve explicit, extensive mandatory religious content integrated throughout the program."

2. *"Faith-centered" organizations* were founded for a religious purpose, and the governing board and almost all staff are required to share the organization's faith commitments. Faith-centered programs include explicit religious messages and activities but are designed so that participants can readily opt out of these activities and still expect positive outcomes.

3. *"Faith-related" organizations* were also founded by religious people, or for a religious purpose, but programs have very little religious content. Clients may be invited to "religious activities outside program parameters" or may "hold informal conversations with staff." The board members may be required or expected to share the founder's faith, and project staff are expected to have "sensitivity to the faith commitment of founders."

4. *"Faith-background" organizations* may have had ties to a faith tradition at one time, but the faith commitment of board and staff members is now not considered relevant. "Faith-background" programs have no explicit religious content and there is "no expectation that religious change is needed for desired outcome."

5. *"Faith-secular partnerships"* have "no explicit reference to religious content" in programs. "Religious change is not necessary for outcomes, but it is expected that the faith of participants from religious partners will add value to the program." Typically, the secular partner drives the partnership, with strong input from the faith partners. Board members and staff are not required to affirm any religious belief or practice.

I want to stress that there is no "right way" to be faith-based. These categories should help you to describe your organization as it exists now, not to judge whether you are "faith-based enough." I have seen faith-based groups of each of the five types do effective work. You can decide where your group fits in the continuum described above by looking at how faith fits into your program content and the characteristics of your organization.

How Faith-Based Are Your Programs?

Looking at the faith elements of your programs is a good first step in assessing the faith-based nature of your organization. As you begin to evaluate your programs, remember: many faith-based groups have a variety of programs, with varying levels of faith content. Perhaps some programs won't have any faith content at all. Within one faith-based organization, for example, you may find an addiction-recovery program that incorporates spiritual conversion, a housing program with no spiritual component, and a program for high school girls with an optional Bible study. As you read through the next few pages, you may see your group in several of the categories.

Make it a practice within your organization to think through how faith is incorporated into your programming and why. The following questions will help you identify how faith fits in your programming:

1. *Do your programs have spiritual content?* Look for the following: Scripture study, prayer, discipleship and spiritual education programs; connection to activities of a particular church congregation; participation in worship services and events. Keep in mind that some of your programs may have spiritual content and others may not, depending on the program outcomes you are trying to achieve.

2. *Are the spiritual aspects of programs optional or mandatory for participants?* Mandatory participation may be appropriate if the desired outcomes are tied to the spiritual growth of the participant. Or you may choose to make spiritual ac-

tivities optional, giving participants a chance to say no when invited. Offering spiritual activities at another time or place is a way to make it clear that they are optional and that participants can decide not to attend if they choose.

3. *Are the outcomes of programs strongly tied to their spiritual content?* Sometimes you can't remove the spiritual content or make it optional and expect to achieve the same outcomes. Some programs within your organization may have to keep the spiritual-development piece intact, because the success of the participants depends on their ability to build and sustain a relationship with God.

4. *Is spiritual content an explicit part of program plans?* Some faith-based groups incorporate the faith aspect into the process of planning their programs. This is a way of formalizing the spiritual component to help ensure that it is included. Other groups keep the planning much more informal, just allowing the spiritual part to happen as it happens.

5. *Are staff and volunteers expected to talk with program participants about faith?* Sometimes the faith component comes through informal relationships with staff members or volunteers, rather than through a formal curriculum or program activity. Some ministry organizations prepare their people for faith conversations with participants and encourage them to look for opportunities to have them. Other groups are much less intentional about this component, just assuming that some conversations about faith will take place along the way.

Having programs all along the faith-based continuum within one organization may be appropriate, giving your organization flexibility to design programs with specific outcomes in mind. For example, some work is much more effective when programs have explicit spiritual content. You could argue that programs that help people overcome addictions have greater impact when participants have a spiritual life and a connection to a faith community.

Some programs achieve better results when secular partners are involved, however. Those partnerships may make it difficult to include specific spiritual content in the program. In my years of work in youth development, for example, I've seen powerful examples of churches and public schools working together to raise student achievement. Public schools (at least the ones I've worked with) are not as open to explicit spiritual content in programs, because of their public funding and the religious diversity in student populations. If we had brought out the Bibles in the public schools we worked with in South Minneapolis, for example, we would have been shown the door promptly.

Depending on the theology and characteristics of your faith-based organization, it may be difficult for your group to develop programs at one or the other end of the continuum. For example, theologically conservative ministries may have difficulty partnering with secular institutions, and more liberal faith-based groups may be reluctant to make the faith component of programs mandatory for participants. However, letting the outcomes you are trying to achieve drive the faith component of your programs will lead you to try approaches that may be more effective over the long term.

How Faith-Based Is Your Organization?

The work done by the Working Group on Human Needs and Faith-Based and Community Initiatives to identify the five types of faith-based groups described above includes an evaluation of organizational characteristics such as mission, funding, and selection of staff, and how those aspects of the organization are tied to faith. I have pulled out seven of the characteristics identified by the working group and developed my own descriptions of them below. I've also added one of my own—involvement of volunteers. Looking at the following eight areas, ask yourself these questions:

1. *Mission statement.* Is the mission of your organization explicitly religious? Perhaps it includes a Scripture reference or uses terms such as "biblical justice" or "evangelism." Or maybe your mission statement is rather neutral, and an outside person wouldn't be able to tell by reading it that your organization is faith-based.

2. *Founding.* Who founded your organization and for what purpose? Your founders may have expressed a strong faith

and brought it into many elements of the organization. Sometimes that faith focus shifts over the years, as staff and board members change and the vision and mission of the organization is modified to meet the changing needs of the community.

3. *Board of directors.* Some faith-based organizations require that board members profess a particular faith, or even that board members affiliate with a particular denomination or congregation. Such a policy may make sense if your faith-based organization's purpose is to build unity and strong working relationships among people of faith or people from particular congregations. Other faith-based groups seek more diversity within their boards, focusing more on program expertise, fundraising ability, and connection to the community as selection criteria.

4. *Selection of senior management.* Another way to be faith-based is to select senior management, at least in part, on the basis of their profession of a particular faith. In most nonprofits, senior management would be the executive director or president of the organization. In larger nonprofits, senior management would also include positions like the chief operating officer and the director of development.

5. *Selection of other staff.* Are other staff members required to express a particular religious faith as well? Some faith-based groups believe the spiritual content of their programs is so important that they want to make sure to hire staff who share those spiritual beliefs and can communicate and teach them effectively. Other faith-based groups take this criterion out of the hiring equation, focusing more on other skills and experiences.

6. *Involvement of volunteers.* Are volunteers also expected to subscribe to a particular faith? Your ministry may want volunteers for your faith-content programs to be able to share the faith from a personal perspective. Or if the organization and some of its programs do not have a spiritual focus, you may decide to welcome volunteers without regard to their spiritual beliefs.

7. *Collaborative partners.* The "faith" in your "faith-based" group might also come from your collaborative partners,

perhaps congregations or faith-based nonprofits that work in the same field as your group. Your faith-based partners may have expectations that will lead your group to include more spiritual content in programming.

8. *Financial support.* As a group, faith-based organizations receive financial support from a broad variety of sources. Some groups prefer to seek support almost exclusively from people of faith and religious institutions, saying that these types of funders are less likely to place limits on the spiritual content of programs. Other faith-based groups like to incorporate secular funders into the mix, seeking grants from foundation, corporate, and government sources and individuals who may not share the religious views of the organization.

What Do Secular Funders Think of Faith-Based Groups?

I've been fundraising long enough to have had some candid conversations with secular funders regarding how they feel about faith-based groups. Churches and ministry groups are definitely on the radar screen for most funders, and foundation and corporate staff members have developed opinions from their dealings with such organizations over the years. Mostly, I hear that secular funders see churches and ministry groups as vital parts of the community, but they become frustrated with these groups too. Here is what I've learned over the years about what secular funders think of faith-based organizations.

What secular funders like about faith-based groups

Faith-based groups have strong ties to the community. Many funders see that churches and ministry organizations have a unique relationship to the communities around them, providing a safe place for community residents to come for help, support, and friendship. This tie to the community puts faith-based groups in a position to do something valuable that other types of institutions might not be able to. For example, churches are often seen by community residents as a place where compassionate people might help them get connected to resources they need such as housing, food, or clothing. Families in crisis might see the church as having a "friendlier face" than a public school, government agency, or secular nonprofit group.

Many funders also see the unique role that congregations can play in calling attention to injustice and organizing people to respond. The prophetic voice of the church can draw people together in powerful ways. And the church can offer a "neutral ground" for those seeking to respond to injustice or a crisis, a place where everyone can come together to talk, grieve, get angry, and decide how to move forward. The congregational role is bigger than simply offering services on site. It can set the agenda for a community and move a broader group of people into action.

It's often the clergy who facilitate the congregation's role in the community, serving as a voice, forming relationships, and building bridges between different constituencies. Ram Cnaan, associate director of the Center for Research on Religion and Urban Civil Society at the University of Pennsylvania, documents the considerable role of clergy and the church in improving the quality of life in communities in his book *The Invisible Caring Hand*:

> Above all, clergy are the gatekeepers of the congregation and also its bridge to the wider society and its many institutions. When public authorities, health planners, political and community organizers, or business interests want access to people in the community, they often must go to the clergy and ask their support.... Similarly, when residents wish to approach larger institutions such as hospitals, city halls, transportation authorities, sheriffs, housing officials, and local businesses, they turn to the clergy as those most likely to be heard and accepted as the leaders of their communities.[2]

Many funders see the important and unique role of clergy in bringing about positive community change, and want to support that role in their grant-making.

Faith-based organizations are effective at reaching communities of color. Involving faith communities is critical to reaching communities of color. Church plays a unique role in many of these communities, serving as a hub for much more than just Sunday worship. In the African American community, for example, church is where many people go for just about everything—finding a job, becoming politically informed and engaged, socializing with friends, and serving the community. Many funders have begun to recognize this role, and see that much good work that needs to be done in communities of color cannot be done without the churches.

In the 20 years that I have been writing grant proposals, I have begun to notice more and more African American and Latino churches from our area on grantee lists. The grants provide support for a wide range of programs, such as addressing youth violence, working with "prisoner reentry" (to society), and reducing health disparities. Funders have begun to realize that to reach many of these communities successfully, the church needs to get involved. Faith communities typically have broad-reaching networks and the ear of the people. Working with the churches is an ideal way to spread the word, get people to participate, and draw in needed partners.

Faith-based organizations have a built-in base of volunteers. Many ministry nonprofits are tied to congregations or denominations that provide a ready base of willing volunteers. Funders see this aspect as a real advantage, and some funding groups have even begun to support efforts to organize and train faith-based volunteers. I have witnessed thousands of Christians mobilized to work in public schools and parks, prisons, youth development organizations, women's shelters, and many other kinds of outreach efforts. Many Christians view working to meet community needs as a matter of living out the Great Commandment. Funders see this pool of volunteers as "added value," something that faith-based organizations bring to the table that other types of nonprofits might not.

The spiritual aspect of faith-based organizations can bring about long-term transformation for the people served. Although some funders get nervous about the spiritual aspect of our work, others see it as a real asset. I've even encountered funders who aren't people of faith themselves who understand that some issues require supernatural intervention and a spiritual focus. For many participants in programs I've been affiliated with, the knowledge that there is a God who loves them, made them unique, and wants the best for them is an important part of their transformation.

Those of us in ministry already know that the spiritual aspect of what we do makes a difference, and a body of research is developing that supports the idea that faith-based approaches may achieve greater results. In the book *Churches That Make a Difference*, Ron Sider and Phil Olson, with Evangelicals for Social Action, and Heidi Rolland Unruh, of Eastern Baptist Theological Seminary, summarize some of the research:

> More and more reports began to surface about the astonishing effectiveness of some faith-based approaches. Studies of Teen Challenge's Christ-centered drug and alcohol rehab program revealed recovery rates far higher than in most secular programs. The Ten Point Coalition, a faith-based response to gang violence led by Rev. Eugene Rivers, has dramatically reduced youth homicides in a gritty Boston neighborhood.
>
> Prison Fellowship has reduced prisoners' recidivism rates. Faith-based mentoring teams seem to have played a crucial role in enabling Ottawa County in Michigan to help every recipient move off the welfare rolls.[3]

Some funders are aware of this research, and you might consider using it as you prepare grant proposals.

Faith-based organizations usually help people no matter who they are. Compassionate hearts and zeal for the Lord have historically led Christians into places and relationships where few others would go. This work continues today, as faith-based ministries deliberately locate in some of the toughest neighborhoods in our nation to form relationships with people whom others have rejected. It's Christians' belief in the "new life" and transformation that helps them take these risks. Because of this willingness to help anyone and everyone, many funders see faith-based groups as a key component of any strategy to meet community needs.

Faith-based organizations are good at building long-term relationships with people. It's easy to look at more money and more programs as the solutions for children and families who are trying to turn the corner. But it's relationships with people who care and who are willing to stick around that make the greatest difference. I have witnessed the power of these relationships as Christians have stepped forward to get to know someone, offering encouragement, accountability, and friendship.

Studies of effective faith-based organizations have shown that these groups can provide more flexible and personally tailored help to families and individuals because they often work on a smaller scale. Instead of serving a large number of individuals with short-term programs, many ministries "go deep" with their participants, providing intensive, one-on-one help over the long term. Building caring relationships between participants and volunteers is often a key part of this approach.

Funders understand the power of these long-term relationships, so be sure to emphasize them as you prepare your proposal.

What secular funders find challenging about faith-based groups

Funders have also talked with me about what they find challenging about faith-based groups.

Church staff are overworked, making it difficult for them to implement new programs. Some of the funders I interviewed expressed concern about how many "hats" pastors and other church staff members wear. Pastors of smaller congregations often have to preach, counsel, run the youth program, visit the sick, clean the church, and drive the bus, among many other duties. The life of a typical youth pastor is often just as complicated. So funders wonder: once staff members have finished the "regular" work of the church, how would they ever find the time to start and run the after-school program?

It's a good question, one you should think about if you work in a church setting. Ask yourself: can our current staff members handle more work in addition to their church duties? If the answer is "no," then strongly consider adding new program directors and other staff to oversee the implementation of new programs.

Faith-based groups intermingle their faith with everything else. Secular funders struggle with this trait because many of them need to consider the faith piece separately, often because their bylaws or guidelines require it. So secular funders get frustrated with ministry groups that see no difference between programs that have spiritual goals and those that don't.

One funder told me that her foundation wanted to support a church that was doing work in the community, but the pastor just could not understand why the funder made a distinction between programs that were set up to evangelize and those that weren't, programs that were only for church members and those that were for the broader community. "It's all the same thing," he kept saying to her. "I don't know what the difference is." Separating out the faith piece is a new way of thinking for many ministry leaders, but they need to do so if they want to partner with secular funders. This approach doesn't mean sifting out the faith piece entirely, just learning to think about it and talk about it differently (see strategy 4 at the end of this chapter).

Some ministry groups are willing to serve only the people from their own congregation or faith tradition. Such a policy is of great concern to funders. Foundations and corporations generally like to put resources toward the broader community good, not toward improving the lot of an exclusive group of people.

Usually faith-based organizations intend to serve a broad group of people, and this distinction isn't really an issue. But I have encountered this exclusive focus when churches seek grant money to fill financial gaps in church ministries. Maybe the youth-group budget is running in the red this year, and you figure that some of your youth events might be of interest to local foundations and corporations. Funders might be interested, but be prepared to be asked about the constituency served by the events. You'll more likely get funded if you target all youth in your geographical area, rather than just the youth of your church.

Leaders and staff of faith-based organizations are too nice in situations where they need to make hard choices. Some faith-based groups focus so much on ministry to people that it is difficult for them to make hard decisions about personnel, programs, or budgets when necessary. It can be difficult to balance the development and nurture of people with bottom-line business practices. For example, how many chances do we give an employee before we let him go? How can we cut a program from the budget when it is definitely helping some people? There is no one right answer for situations like this, but I think faith-based groups tend to base decisions too much on what's good for one or two people, and not enough on what's good for the whole organization.

One funder told me: "When I worked in the corporate world, employees would generally get three chances. But somehow in ministry, we feel we have to be 'extra nice,' giving a person seventy-times-seven chances! Ministry groups shouldn't leave ineffective employees in the organization. If they're 'dead weight,' they should be removed. Anything else is poor stewardship." Funders will expect your group to be able to make the hard choices when necessary.

Faith-based organizations often lack administrative and management capacity. Any nonprofit group, faith-based or not, can struggle with management issues like raising sufficient funds and attracting qualified staff. Faith-based organizations seem to have a greater struggle here—perhaps it's that most faith leaders got into the work because of their ability to minister effectively. They have a passion for comforting and counseling the sick, the elderly, and the disadvantaged. But they didn't expect to have to read financial reports, file IRS forms, or write grant proposals as a part of the job. Seminary programs designed to prepare people to lead ministries tend to focus only on the ministry end of things. I frequently hear pastors say how little they learned in seminary about the business-management side of ministry.

If your nonprofit organization struggles with management issues, consider getting some training in nonprofit management before pursuing grant funding. Most communities have organizations that provide training in fundraising, financial management, governance issues, human resources management, and other nonprofit issues.

Faith-based organizations don't understand the corporate and foundation funding process. Though some of the most well-resourced nonprofits in this country are faith-based, many faith-based groups are less sophisticated than other types of nonprofits when it comes to understanding the fine points of the grant-making business. I've encountered plenty of faith-based groups that just didn't seem to understand that each funder has established a process for seeking a grant—a format for a proposal, deadlines to meet, and a group of people who review and respond. This lack of sophistication can be frustrating for funders when faith-based organizations don't assemble the proposal correctly and don't respect the funder's carefully developed process.

If you are new to fundraising, reading this book is a good first step, but you may need some additional education to help prepare you to seek grants. I've listed other written resources in the bibliography. You may also want to seek out grantwriting training through organizations in your area.

Advice about Approaching Secular Funders

These next sections offer specific advice on how you can approach secular funders. Take a step back and consider this advice before you move into a conversation with a secular funder.

Decide whether this funder is a fit for your program and organization. Sometimes you have to say no. You may research a secular funder and decide that the funder's terms just won't work for your ministry. If your ministry has a spiritual component that is woven into the program, secular funding is probably not an option. Or you may find that some secular funders are uncomfortable with informal spiritual content, or a connection to a particular church congregation, or a requirement that all board members express a Christian faith.

Often you can determine whether there is a fit between the program and the funder by reading the funder's guidelines and annual report, or by having a phone conversation with a staff person. Sometimes, however, the lack of fit won't become evident until after you've submitted a proposal and have subsequent conversations. Whenever it becomes apparent that the funder wants something very different from what you do, you should end the process.

Never hide your faith. Don't try to act as though you're not faith-based if you are. Be honest with funders about the role of faith for your group. If you are connected to a particular church or denomination, say so. If most of your volunteers come from local faith communities, say that too. And, of course, if the spiritual component is an integral part of your programming that cannot be separated out, you have to communicate that to the funder, or you risk entering into a dishonest funding relationship.

Never ask the funder for permission to conduct spiritual activities. Funders aren't setting the agenda for your organization; you are. It is dangerous to put any funder in a "permission-giving" role. Don't ever approach a funder and ask questions like this: "Would it be all right for us to do Bible study?" or "If we pray with folks, would that be a problem?"

Put yourself in the driver's seat on this issue, and using the tools on the previous pages, decide first what you mean when you say your organization is faith-based. This exercise will help you identify how important the faith and spiritual components are to you and whether they can in any way be separated from the rest of your program. Once you have done that work, you are prepared to talk to a secular funder.

Anticipate objections about the faith component and respond to them up front. If you know you are approaching a funder who has concerns about your faith aspect, respond to potential concerns in the body of the grant proposal. Be truthful, of course, but provide as many reassurances as you can. For example, many funders have concerns that faith-based organizations will provide services only to people from their particular church or religious faith. If that's not the case for you, include language like this in your proposal: "Our nonprofit organization was founded by Christians, but it serves a broad range of community members who subscribe to a wide range of beliefs." As you think through the objections funders may have about your ministry, review the list of "What secular funders find challenging about faith-based groups" above. Depending on how you implement the spiritual aspect of your programs, you may also be able to tell funders that the spiritual component is optional or that it is underwritten by other funders.

It is often appropriate to talk with funders about your own motivations for being involved in the ministry. Reflections on your own faith journey and how you became involved with your ministry organization can fit very easily into a conversation with a funder. Such a discussion can be a great way for you to share your own witness and may bolster your funding request as you talk about the strength of your faith and how it has led you forward. I think too often we think we can't be ourselves around funders. This simply isn't true. As people of faith, we shouldn't try to hide our faith or leave it out of the picture just because we are asking for money. One caution: I wouldn't let the description of your faith journey be the main focus of the conversation. After all, the funder is there to take a look at your programs and decide whether to fund them.

Strategies for Approaching Secular Funders

I've identified four strategies that could work as you approach secular funders. Keep in mind that one strategy won't fit all funders. Each corporation and foundation is unique, and you should read each funder's guidelines carefully before choosing the strategy that you think would be most effective.

Strategy 1: Describe your ministry the way you see fit, and don't change a thing. Sometimes faith-based groups feel called to describe themselves in their own language, leaving in all of the spiritual wording and content and taking their chances with the funders' response. This option is more about the language being used than anything else. I've found that people in ministry frequently have a particular way of talking. They use terms such as "new life in Christ" and "equipping the body of Christ." The value of this strategy is that you are as authentic as you can be when describing the work you do, and you don't worry about what the funder wants to hear. The disadvantage, of course, is that you may alienate funders who are concerned about their money going to the spiritual aspects of programs, as well as funders who don't understand or who are confused by spiritual language.

Strategy 2: Exclude the spiritual aspect from the proposal. Another option to consider is excluding the spiritual aspect from the proposal entirely. This approach works only if the spiritual aspect is minimal or if you believe that you can clearly separate it from the rest of your program. Otherwise, you risk being dishonest with the funder, an act that may result in rejection of your grant and damage to your reputation in the funding community. Keep in mind that funders do talk with each other, so your dishonesty with one may affect your ability to get grants from other funders as well.

Some scenarios where it might work to leave the spiritual aspect out of the proposal entirely include these:

- Your transitional housing program invites participants to an optional weekly Bible study sponsored by another organization. It's made clear to participants that they are not required to attend.
- Your arts center sponsors an exhibit of art with spiritual themes that is open to the entire community.
- Your youth center teaches a curriculum to kids based on biblical concepts, but Bible passages themselves are not a part of the teaching. Youth consider how to be kind and honest, respect their parents, and encourage each other.

Of course, if your organization is a congregation, funders may still ask you about the spiritual component of your programs, even if it isn't mentioned in your proposal. Funders may assume that the congregational connection automatically means faith content. You could anticipate these questions by addressing the issue directly in your proposal, describing the nature of the relationship with the congregation and how faith figures into program content.

Strategy 3: Find other funding for the spiritual aspect of the program. Separating out the spiritual aspect of your program and seeking other funding for it is another approach that can help attract secular funding. Under this strategy, the spiritual component of your program is optional for participants and is completely funded by other sources, perhaps by churches or individual donors. This approach assures a foundation or corporation that its funding will not be used for activities like Bible study or discipleship groups.

I would recommend that you still include the spiritual aspect of the program in the narrative of your proposal, in the interest of being totally honest with the funder. However, you can describe it briefly using terms that will be understood by the funder. (For example, leave out the heavy-duty theological language.)

In the budget for your proposal, you can still show the cost of the spiritual component. Just clearly separate the costs and funding for it, showing that it is distinct from the other components of the program. Be sure to include all costs of the spiritual component, including staff time devoted to it (and a corresponding portion of benefits), supplies, use of space, transportation, and a portion of your administrative expenses and overhead as well.

Strategy 4: Leave the spiritual aspect in the proposal, but describe it differently. This strategy involves describing the spiritual or faith component of your program in terms that would be understood by and would not threaten secular funders. *This is a change in language, not program content.*

As Christians, we can have the tendency to lapse into "church-speak," describing everything in biblical or theological terms. This kind of language could be a hindrance to you as you seek funding from secular funders. First, you may give the impression that one of the primary objectives of your work is evangelistic, even when that is not the case. Second, you may confuse or threaten foundation staff members who don't have a church or theological background.

This strategy assumes that there is more than one way to talk about almost everything, and that changing your language can help open doors to conversations and potential funding. I have frequently used this strategy, and when I do, I always think about the apostle Paul in Athens. Paul told the same story everywhere he went but altered his language to fit the context and the audience.

If you'd like to use this strategy, get someone outside your ministry group to read your proposal and point out the places where you use faith language. Often it can be helpful to find someone who is not a Christian or who has some distance from the ministry world. That person's perspective will be different from the one you get inside your ministry group. Then you can find a different way to describe the same thing.

Here are some examples of how you might use different language to describe your faith-based program:

Remove language like this	*Replace it with language like this*
Bible study	Spiritual development
Prayer	Character-building activities
Proclaiming the gospel	(avoid language about evangelism)
Equipping the body of Christ	Recruiting and training volunteers
Pastoral counseling	Counseling and support groups
Christ-centered programs	Church-sponsored programs
Showing the love of Jesus Christ	Acting out our faith

No Compromise

The ultimate goal of ministry fundraising is to secure funding for your organization *without* compromising your mission and values. The tools and information in this chapter are offered with that goal in mind, not to encourage you to bend your organization or its programs to fit the mold of secular funders. You may decide after reading this chapter that secular funders are not a good fit for your ministry. That's a positive outcome, since it helps you focus your efforts on funders that are the best fit for your group. Or reading this chapter may lead you to decide that you'd like to try to develop partnerships with secular funders. The very process of trying to form these partnerships can lead to positive outcomes as well, forcing examination of values and serving to clarify how faith is incorporated into your organization.

Key Questions

1. What makes your organization faith-based?

2. If your programs have spiritual content, is it:

   - Optional or mandatory for participants?
   - A major part of the program?
   - Strongly tied to program outcomes?

3. For what aspects of your ministry would you seek secular funding?

4. Which of the four strategies for approaching secular funders would your group be likely to use? Why?

   - *Strategy 1*: Describe your ministry the way you see fit and don't change a thing.
   - *Strategy 2*: Exclude the spiritual aspect from the proposal entirely.

- *Strategy 3*: Find other funding for the spiritual aspect of the program.
- *Strategy 4*: Leave the spiritual aspect in the proposal, but describe it differently.

_____
_____
_____
_____

6

Finding and Studying the Funder

A key part of the grantwriting process is like detective work—searching out possible funders for your ministry and finding out everything you can about them. I describe many tools in this chapter that will help you in this process of finding and studying the funder.

Find the Funder

Just how do you track down the foundations and corporations that would fund a group like yours? When I first started in fundraising, I believed that somewhere there was a magic list of all the funders who would just love to give to our organization. As I consult with ministry groups on fundraising, I find that many other people believe in that list as well.

There isn't such a list. Finding funders takes discipline. It's hard work. And it's something you can learn how to do. Once you start the hunt for funders, you will begin to notice how much information is out there on who gives money to what. To find that information, you need to get into the mind-set of "the search"; listening to what people say, making connections in your own networks, and asking around about funding opportunities. Start your search for grants in the networks that are closest to you—your faith community and the people already connected to your organization, such as board members and volunteers.

Your faith community

If your ministry is connected to a church or a group of churches, you may be able to connect with funders through the people within those congregations. The first step is to communicate regularly with the people in the church about your organization, its accomplishments, and its needs. You can stay in touch through written materials such as a newsletter or brochure, or through face-to-face contact in Sunday services or other types of church meetings. Whenever you talk with the people in your partner churches, be sure that they have the opportunity to sign up to receive more information and to send in their own contributions. Including a response envelope with any material you distribute will give people an opportunity to respond. This is a great way to build your mailing list and your individual donor base.

The next step, once the people in the church have a good understanding of who you are and what you do, is to ask people to tell you whether they are connected to any funders. To find corporate and foundation contacts within your faith community, let people know you are looking for them. Whenever you have a speaking engagement, talk about the support you've received from XYZ Foundation and what a help it's been. Then encourage folk who work for corporations or have other connections to funders to come and talk with you afterward.

Another tool I've used is a bulletin insert that asks people to identify their employers. You can then look through the companies listed in the inserts and compare them to your grants index and the funding lists from other organizations, tools that are described in the next few pages. I found a vice president of a large corporation through a bulletin insert at one of the churches where I worked. She helped us secure larger grants from her company and eventually served as the chair of the board of directors of our nonprofit group.

Your volunteers

Your board members and other volunteers in your organization might also be able to find potential grant opportunities for your ministry. Often a connection is made when one of your board members or volunteers works at a corporation in your area and connects you with giving opportunities through the company. These folk might also make connections with family foundations or community foundations, usually through a friend or colleague who works there.

To encourage your board members and volunteers to uncover funding opportunities for you, you need to tell them what you are looking for. Tell them what types of corporate gifts are helpful to your ministry and remind them, for example, that their company may have a grants program. Then they will be primed to respond when an announcement about a grant opportunity comes across their desk at work. Several times in my career, volunteers came forward with funding announcements that were not distributed to the general public. That is, only employees of the corporation were notified, and it was up to them to find nonprofits with which to share the information. One ministry I worked for received a large grant this way, only because an employee brought the opportunity to our attention and put in a good word for us.

Other organizations' funding lists

One of the best ways to find out who is funding what is to look at the annual reports or newsletters of groups similar to yours. Most nonprofits issue a report to their constituents each year, and it typically includes a list of foundations, corporations, individuals, and other funding sources who have made gifts to the organization.

Choose groups that have a similar mission and are about the same size as your group. For example, if you have just formed a nonprofit focused on the health needs of low-income children in your area, you might research the funding lists of nonprofits that have health programs, including ministry groups. Because you are new and small, getting information on the health outreach program run by the local neighborhood association might generate more appropriate funders than researching the funders of your local hospital, an organization much larger than yours.

This research technique works best if you can get the annual reports of five to ten relevant nonprofits and look for funders that

appear in several reports. This process can surface funders that
aren't listed in grants indexes because they are not required to publish a lot of information about themselves, such as corporate giving
programs.

Grant indexes

Grant indexes may also be helpful in your hunt for funders. The
best kind of index focuses on funders that are nearby and that give
to groups in your geographic area. Such indexes are often published by the local council on foundations. These councils function
as trade associations for funders and can provide useful resources
for grant seekers through their Web sites, training programs, and
published materials. Look for your local council on foundations
at the Giving Forum Web site (www.givingforum.org), and then
contact your local council to see if it publishes an index. Keep in
mind that a grant index probably won't contain information on
individual donors and may not include information on some corporate giving programs either.

Grants indexes usually have an entry for each funder that includes the following information:

Name of funder
Address
Phone number
Web site address
Contact person and his or her phone number and e-mail address
A list of funding priorities
Program limitations and restrictions, including types of activi-
ties the funder will *not* support
The geographic focus of the funder
Intended beneficiaries
Application information
Preferred form of initial contact
Grant deadlines
Whether the group accepts the common grant application used
in your area
Who makes the funding decisions

How long it takes for a proposal to be reviewed

A short list of sample grants. The index entry may list five or six groups (or a few more) that the funder has supported, giving you an initial impression of whom they give to and how much they give (but you'll want to research this further).

Financial information, including the funder's assets, grants paid out the previous year, the number of grants, and the range of grants (largest to smallest). This tells you what size funder you are looking at, giving you a sense of how much to ask for and whether the funder supports a broad range of nonprofits or a short, exclusive list of organizations.

One of the most valuable parts of a grants index can be the list of funders organized by interest areas and types of grants made, such as education or health or the environment. A quick look at that list may lead you to five or ten funders worth researching further. Other sections of the index may list organizations that provide capital grants, general operating funds, or in-kind gifts.

Another tool that you may find in the back of the book: a list of the trustees of all of the funders indexed in the book. Trustees are board members of foundations and are typically involved in making funding decisions. You, your board members, and other volunteers can peruse the list for trustees you know. Having these connections inside a funding organization may help your grant proposal get a better hearing.

Online grant indexes

Some grant indexes are available online, usually for an annual subscription fee. You may also consider subscribing to a grant-search Web site, which can lead you to potential funders and to other Web sites, depending on the type of grant you are seeking. Online products are often updated on a regular basis and are generally more current than printed grant indexes. Online subscriptions may also provide you with more ways to search for and sort funders than a printed index would. These advantages come with a cost, however, as the fee for these subscriptions is usually more (sometimes much more) than you would pay for resources in book form. Again, finding an online tool that focuses on your local area is preferable to accessing one that covers national funders, unless you plan to work on a national level.

Training events

There may be seminars or conferences that highlight the major funders in your area, providing information on their priorities and application processes. Your local council on foundations may host an event like this periodically, called something like "The Top 50 Foundations in New York," for example. Such seminars may be taught by seasoned fundraisers in your area who can give you the inside scoop on how local funders operate.

Mass media

Pay attention to the news, and you'll likely find a few possible funders for your organization. Read articles about foundations and corporations in your area and what they are supporting. Corporations, in particular, seek news coverage, since part of the purpose of their giving is to enhance the public image of the company. You'll also want to read articles about major new initiatives or fundraising campaigns launched by nonprofits in your area. The religion page or section of your newspaper may also have relevant information.

Study the Funder

Suppose you've used the tips above to surface 20 funders that look to be a potential fit for your health ministry. What do you do now? You may be tempted to send out the same proposal to all 20 funders, but that is not the best strategy. Once a foundation or corporation ends up on your "potential" list, you need to study it to determine how well it fits your organization and how to craft a proposal that will have the best possible chance of being funded. As you use the tools I've identified below, look for the following information on potential funders:

- size of the grants given out by the funder
- grant deadlines
- what the funder is interested in
- proposal requirements (what you need to send in)
- whether the funder supports faith-based organizations

This step is critical, so give it your best effort.

Funding Guidelines

Corporate and foundation funders produce guidelines about their priorities and processes, and those guidelines might include all the information you need to begin your study. Usually the funder has a Web site, and you can find the guidelines there. Or call, and you can get a printed copy by mail.

The guidelines are a "must-read" before you write your grant proposal. They identify what the funder supports and doesn't support, and the process for seeking a grant. Read the guidelines carefully before contacting the funder with questions about the grants and the proposal process, matters that may well be addressed in the guidelines. If you don't read the guidelines, you run the risk of (1) irritating the funder with questions you could easily have answered with a glance at the guidelines, or (2) sending in a proposal that is irrelevant to the funder. You also demonstrate that you are not thorough and detail-oriented, an impression that may call into question the capacity of your organization. To me, submitting a proposal without reading the guidelines is like proposing marriage to someone you've never met. It makes no sense to propose a partnership when you know nothing about your potential partner.

If you are proposing an innovative program that has not been tried before or you are addressing an issue that is new in your community, it's possible you will not see your ideas reflected in any of the funder guidelines you read. For example, your group might be the first one to provide programs and services to a new wave of immigrants just beginning to arrive in your town. If the funders in your area haven't yet made immigrant programs a priority, you'll need to begin to build relationships with funders to make the case for your new idea. Start with people you know—talk to foundation staff you already know and ask for suggestions on what you can do, whom else you can talk to. You might consider bringing along other nonprofit or ministry leaders who have the same ideas, so they can add their voices to the conversation.

Persuading funders to expand their guidelines or to take on a new program area can be a slow process, but don't be discouraged. I'm aware of many trailblazing nonprofit leaders who eventually convinced funders of the wisdom of supporting a new community issue or program model. Often, an overall change in the funding community begins with just one foundation staff member who begins to advocate for an issue among his or her peers. In my community, early childhood education has become a top priority for many funders, largely because a small group of nonprofit leaders and one foundation program officer began working on the issue decades ago.

Typical Funder Guidelines

When you locate the guidelines for a particular funder, you can expect them to include the following kinds of information. I've included quotations from the published guidelines of several funders, so you can get a sense of the language used by foundations and corporations to communicate their priorities and processes.

Interest areas of the funder

The guidelines will identify the funder's areas of interest. Most foundations and corporations have decided how they will focus their giving efforts, usually on community needs and issues as well as the interests of the leaders of the foundation or corporation. Interest areas could include a focus on youth development, housing, the arts, or religion, for example.

This part of the guidelines may also list certain approaches or types of programming that the foundation prefers. For example, under youth development, the funder may list youth centers, mentoring programs, and academic enrichment. The more specific the list, the better, because it gives you a much better idea of whether your group fits or not.

The Joyce Foundation, a family foundation based in Chicago, focuses on improving the quality of life in the Great Lakes Area—Illinois, Indiana, Michigan, Minnesota, Ohio, and Wisconsin. The foundation devotes its resources to public-policy advocacy, rather than to direct service. The interest areas for the foundation are education, employment, environment, gun violence, money and politics, and culture. The guidelines include subcategories and detailed descriptions for each of these interests. For example, the teacher-quality subcategory is described as follows:

> The Foundation supports efforts to improve federal, state, and district policies so that high-need schools in Chicago, Cleveland, and Milwaukee can attract and retain first-rate teachers. Efforts include research, policy development, model programs, advocacy, and evaluation related to:
>
> - Reform of recruiting and hiring systems
> - Reform of teacher evaluation and compensation systems
> - New teacher support
> - Alternative routes to teaching
> - Principal quality[1]

In contrast, the Lilly Endowment focuses on religion and specifically seeks to enhance and support the quality of ministry in American congregations. The guidelines specify:

> The Endowment has focused on supporting programs and projects that address four broad questions: How do we identify, recruit and call forth a new generation of talented Christian pastors? How do we best prepare and train new ministers for effective and faithful pastoral leadership? How do we improve the skills and sustain the excellence of pastors currently serving congregations? What are basic questions about the current state of the practice of ministry that we need to answer to improve the quality of ministry?[2]

The guidelines go on to give more background on how the endowment views grant-making in this area and what drives its funding decisions. Then you'll see the specifics—how these broad goals and values have been developed into several funding programs, targeted at particular populations and activities:

National Clergy Renewal Program
Clergy Renewal Program for Indiana Congregations
Theological Programs for High School Youth
Programs for the Theological Exploration of Vocation
Transition-into-Ministry
Sustaining Pastoral Excellence[3]

These interest areas and funding programs are specific and will help you determine whether you fit the geographic focus, the target audience, and the types of programming supported by the Lilly Endowment.

Geographic focus of the funder

Funders may focus their grant-making within a geographic area. Corporate funders usually concentrate on communities where their headquarters, plants, and offices are located. Family foundations may make grants primarily in areas where family members have lived or are now living. Community foundations may have been founded to provide resources in the geographic area where they are based—the Philadelphia Foundation and the Minneapolis Foundation, for example.

Like many large corporations, General Mills focuses charitable giving on geographic areas where company offices, plants, and employees are located. The General Mills Foundation guidelines describe the company's decentralized approach to making grants, which includes employees from many company sites around the country:

The General Mills Foundation is based in Minneapolis at the General Mills World Headquarters. In communities around the United States where General Mills has operations, employee volunteers serve on Community Action Councils that work with the Foundation. These councils review funding applications in their communities and suggest projects that meet Foundation funding guidelines.[4]

Translation: if you live in a community with a General Mills presence, this foundation could be a great funding prospect for you.

Demographic focus

You may also see a list of the categories of people that the funder wants to see helped through the grants it makes. People may be identified by age group, ethnicity, gender, economic status, or health status, for example.

Some funders serve a broad demographic. Others concentrate on specific groups, such as "children under the age of 12 who live in urban neighborhoods" or "Native Americans who live on reservations in South Dakota." If you notice this type of specific language, pay close attention to it, because the funder has obviously gone to great trouble to develop a focus on a particular constituency.

The Sheltering Arms Foundation focuses its grant-making on children, and describes its demographic focus as follows:

> The Foundation supports programs benefiting children and their families in Minnesota who are most vulnerable, have least access to resources, and are least likely to have a wide array of choices about their future.[5]

This sentence gives you a great deal of information—who is the focus of the foundation (children), the situation they are in (poverty), as well as the geographic focus of the funder (Minnesota).

Types of grants the funder makes

How does the funder want to see grant money used? Some funders give *unrestricted grants* for general operating expenses, allowing the grantee to decide how the money is spent. But more and more funders are putting their resources into *program grants* designated for one particular project or program. Some funders make *capital grants,* providing resources for bricks-and-mortar building projects or major equipment purchases. And some foundations and corporations give *capacity-building grants,* underwriting strategic planning or staff training, for example,.

Organizational characteristics the funder is looking for

Some funders include a paragraph in their guidelines that describes preferences they have with regard to organizational issues or characteristics. As described in chapter 4, "What Do Funders Really Want?" most funders look to support nonprofits that are run by competent people, that have a track record of success, and that are financially solvent. Some funders look for additional organizational characteristics in their grantees. For example, you may find language that indicates that the funder supports only groups that:

- have 501(c)3 status under the Internal Revenue Service code.
- are small and have budgets under a certain amount.
- are well-established and have been operating at least a certain number of years.
- have involved participants or community residents in their planning processes.
- have written a strategic plan.
- involve employees of the corporation (for corporate funders).

The Mustard Seed Foundation, based in Arlington, Virginia, for example, describes its organizational preferences in a section of its guidelines called "Goals and Biases." One preference concerns "Local church accountability and investment":

> We expect to see a financial investment in the project by the local
> church and view such an investment as a primary indicator to us
> of the significance, accountability, and sustainability of any project. While we participate in the work of parachurch organizations,

we typically do so only in partnership with local churches, matching their financial investment in the project.[6]

Translation: this funder believes so strongly in the work of the
local church that it requires prospective grantees to be supported
by a church, so that the project is sustainable over the long term.

What the funder won't support

Funding guidelines will usually include a list of activities the funder
does not support as well. Be sure to read this section, too. If your
mission or programs are on this "won't fund" list, you know that
you don't have to waste your time sending in a proposal and can
focus on more productive funding options.

Some funders have this phrase (or something like it) written
into their guidelines: "no funding to religious organizations for religious purposes." Reading that might make you believe that there
is no hope for your group to get a grant, but this statement usually
means that a funder is open to providing support to faith-based organizations, just not for any project with spiritual content. As I describe more fully in chapter 5, it can be difficult for people of faith
to separate the spiritual from the nonspiritual aspects of their programs. But you will need to be prepared to do this if you see that
phrase or something similar in a funder's guidelines and you want
to submit a grant. In my experience, many funders want to make
sure that participants in programs they fund aren't coerced into
religious participation that might include Scripture study, prayer,
worship, or attendance at a particular congregation. See page 95 for
strategies on approaching secular funders.

The grant-seeking process

Most funding guidelines also describe how to approach the funder
for a grant. Read this part carefully, as well, so that you don't leave
something out of your proposal that the funder clearly asks for.
Some funders require that you send a letter of inquiry first, before
submitting a full proposal. A letter of inquiry is typically a two- to

four-page summary of a proposal idea. If funders like your idea, they will request that you prepare a full proposal. See page 144 for more information on preparing a letter of inquiry.

Most funders indicate clearly in their guidelines the date by which you must submit your grant proposal. Deadlines vary widely among funders. Some have one deadline a year; others take applications quarterly or have ongoing deadlines (meaning you can submit anytime). Note whether the deadline is a postmark deadline or a deadline by which your application needs to be in the foundation offices. Most funders have strict rules about what happens to proposals that come in late. Typically, they return late proposals without considering them, or just throw them away.

For your full grant proposal, many foundations and corporations now use a common grant application—a standardized cover sheet and outline that can be sent to most funders. A sample of a common grant application is printed in appendix 1. But some funders request additional material as well. You may find that the funder you are approaching asks for the following in addition to the common grant application:

- a copy of your latest newsletter or annual report.
- a copy of your strategic plan or information on your planning processes.
- a list of other, similar organizations doing work in your area.
- if you are requesting a capital grant, a copy of your building plans and information on the site you have selected.

Information may also be included in this part of the guidelines about the format you are expected to use in preparing your application. There may be a page limit and a required font size or margin size for the page. Pay attention here, to ensure that your proposal isn't disqualified on a technicality. You may also be asked to submit multiple copies of your entire proposal or of certain parts of it. Also, be sure to check whether the funder accepts applications online or by e-mail. Some foundations and corporations have shifted to accepting applications electronically, while others still like to receive the paper grant application through the U.S. mail (or another

Exercise: Assessing Your Fit with the Funder

As I review guidelines for a particular funder, I like to use the list of questions in the exercise below to help me assess whether the funder is a good fit for our group. The questions can also help you identify what information you need that the funder does not provide, so that you'll know which questions to ask when you do contact the funder.

- Does your ministry fit the geographic focus of the funder?
- Does your ministry fit the program focus of the funder (housing, youth development, or violence prevention, for example)?
- Does your proposal fit with the group of people the funder wants to serve (preschool children, people with AIDS, the elderly, or chemically dependent adults, for example)?
- Would this funder provide the type of grant you need (general operating, program, capital, capacity-building)?
- What does the appearance of the guidelines and annual report (graphic design, photos, level of detail in the text, and so forth) indicate about the funder's values?
- In the case of a corporate funder, is employee involvement important? If so, do you have an employee of the company involved with your ministry?
- What is the average size of the grants given to programs like yours?
- Can you provide the information the funder is requesting?
- When are the deadlines for receiving proposals, and can you meet them?

carrier that confirms delivery). Pay attention to these details to avoid having your organization's proposal knocked out of consideration.

This part of the guidelines also usually describes the review process for the grant—who reads it first, to whom it gets passed on, and who makes the final decision. There may also be information here on how long the review process takes and when decisions will be made.

A funder's annual report or list of grantees

The annual report or list of grantees details who received grants from the funder and the amounts given to them during a specific time period. Most funders issue a list like this once a year; some update it frequently on their Web site.

This list, when it is available, is another "must read" for you as you prepare your grant application. By looking at the list of grantees, you can find out critical information about a funder that might not be obvious from reading the guidelines. One large corporate funder I have worked with has an official policy of not making capital grants, but its list of grantees shows otherwise. I've found this inconsistency between the guidelines and the actual grant-making to be fairly unusual, but it does happen, making it worthwhile to review both the guidelines and the list of grantees for each funder.

By reading the annual report or list of grantees, you may be able to discover the following information about a funder:

1. *Whether a funder will support start-up organizations or prefers more established groups.* In looking at the list, it won't be immediately obvious to you which ones are the start-up groups. However, if a funder has an entire list full of groups like the Boy Scouts, Catholic Charities, and your local university, you might get the sense that they prefer groups with a track record. That's good news for you if you've been around awhile, but maybe not a good fit if your group is relatively new.

2. *The types of nonprofit organizations supported.* Beyond the interest areas in the funder's guidelines, you might be able

to see more in the grantee list about the types of nonprofits the funder prefers. Does the funder like grassroots groups? Is it interested in organizations run by and for people of color? You might see preferences in the list for large (or small) organizations, nonprofits that organize themselves in particular ways (like neighborhood associations), or groups that engage in certain kinds of activities like community organizing or advocacy. Also, be sure to check whether any faith-based groups are on the grantee list.

3. *The size of gifts made to groups similar to yours.* When I first started fundraising, I'd look at foundation annual reports and get excited about the gazillion dollars that a foundation gave to the United Way or to the local symphony orchestra's capital campaign, probably the largest gifts given out by the funder that year. I thought: "Wow, we can get a grant that big too!"

   I learned that a better measure is to find organizations on the list that are of a size similar to yours in budget, staffing, and scope of programs. If you look through the entire list of grants, you'll probably get a fairly good sense of whether the funder would be likely to give you $1,000, $10,000 or $25,000. Your grant application should always include a request for a specific amount of money, and coming up with a number that is close to what the funder might actually give shows you've done your research. It will also increase your chances of landing a grant.

4. *Whether a funder supports faith-based groups.* If a corporation or foundation makes no specific mention of faith-based organizations in its guidelines, looking at the grantee list can help you learn about the funder's level of interest. If you see lots of churches and ministry groups on the list, then you know that the funder has a pretty high comfort level with faith-based organizations. Just be sure to check what it is that the funder is supporting. The money may be going toward nonreligious programs, like housing or youth programs, which fit in with the foundation's overall guidelines.

Information from grantees

Substantial information about a funder can also come from people you know in other nonprofits who work on fundraising. People who have submitted proposals to a particular funder, especially those who have received funding, can be a great source of advice as you get ready to write your grant request. Generally, nonprofit fundraisers and executive directors like to keep their funding secrets to themselves. So you wouldn't want to ask someone you barely know to tell you everything about her funding sources or how he got a funder to give. However, once you make friends with some of your colleagues in the nonprofit sector, you may be able to share information about funders with each other that will be mutually beneficial.

Develop relationships with nonprofit colleagues who have been around the sector for awhile. Look for seasoned executive directors, development directors, or pastors who serve organizations that secure funding from the outside community. They may be happy to share with you, a relative beginner at grantwriting, what certain funders look for, what their program officers are like, and what to emphasize in your proposal. As you really get to know people, they may even be willing to suggest certain funders to approach.

Guidestar

Guidestar is a Web site (www.guidestar.org) that features financial and program information on more than 1.5 million IRS-recognized nonprofits in the United States. You can register for the basic level of Guidestar for free, but there is a fee for the "fancier" search and data tools available on the Web site. The basic level of Guidestar allows you to look at the 990 form for any IRS-recognized foundation.

The 990 form lists all grants made by a foundation in the previous year. If you are researching a funder that doesn't publish its list of grantees, the 990 form allows you to review the types of organizations funded and the amounts given to each. Many of these 990 forms take a long time to download, particularly for a large foundation, and they're often long, so I recommend scanning 990 forms on the Internet and making notes about giving patterns you see for each funder, rather than printing the forms.

The 990 form also includes information about the total assets of the funder, the total amount distributed during a given fiscal year, officers and directors of the foundation, and where the foundation's money is invested.

You may not want to subscribe to "higher" levels of Guidestar if you already have a grants index that you like (either a paper or online version). Keep in mind that corporate-giving programs that are not organized as foundations are not listed on Guidestar. Individual donors aren't either.

Browsing the Internet

Once you have the name of a potential funder, type it into your Internet browser and see what pops up. The list may include organizations the funder supports. This information can be particularly useful to you if the funder does not issue an annual report or a list of grantees. Take a look at several of these entries and begin to make your own list of grantees, along with the amounts given to each group. You may be able to plot the funder's giving patterns, such as the types of groups supported, the kinds of grants made, and the amounts given.

Your Internet search may also lead you to articles about the funder, organizations that the funder partners with, and the corporation where the foundation or giving program is based. This additional information can give you insight into the values that inform the funder's giving.

One thing I like about doing research on the Internet is that it can pull out information from several years back, giving you more of a historical sense of the funder you are researching. You may find old articles or information about the funder's giving priorities, changes in staffing, even scandals or controversies. Just be sure that you have the most current guidelines and annual report from the funder when you prepare your grant proposal.

Researching funders that don't tell you much about themselves

Some funders are elusive, not publishing much about themselves or seeking public attention for the contributions they make. This can be particularly true of corporate-giving programs that are not organized as foundations. These types of funders are not required by law to disclose what they fund, so unless they choose to tell you through their own guidelines or annual report, it may be difficult to find out.

It can be frustrating to gather information on "elusive" funders, so you'll need to be creative and persistent. You may first find out about such a funder through the annual reports or newsletters of groups similar to yours. Once you have the funder's name, do an Internet search, as I've outlined above. Ask around to see what other folk in ministry groups and nonprofits know about the funder. Your friends and colleagues might tell you about the application process, the size of grants, and the interest areas of the foundation or corporation.

Finally, you'll want to attempt to make personal contact with a funder like this, to fill in information you haven't been able to turn up elsewhere. Some funders are hidden for a reason: they just don't want to talk to anyone! If you sense that is the case, then you may just have to do your best with the information you've gathered to that point. You may wonder: "What are my chances with a funder that doesn't want to talk to me?" A funder like this may be more than happy to review proposals but just recoil from the phone calls and other inquiries that come with being a funder. While your chances are probably better with a funder that you have some personal contact with, don't discount some of these smaller funders that are more hidden. I have received grants from several over the years.

Contacting the Funder

Once you have read everything that the funder has put out about itself and reviewed the information you have gathered on your own, you should contact the staff member or program officer to ask about submitting a request. In my experience, most funders welcome contacts from prospective applicants. They like to be available to answer questions. They will also give you feedback on your idea and tips on submitting your proposal. The exception is the very small foundation without paid staff; there may not be anyone for you to contact. If a foundation like that seems to be a good fit, you may just have to make your best guess based on the funder's written materials.

Here are some tips for contacting a funder:

1. *Keep your side of things short and to the point.* Foundation staff members are typically so busy that they usually don't have time for lengthy phone calls or e-mails.
2. *Ask specific questions,* demonstrating that you did read the funder's materials before you called or e-mailed.
3. *Run your idea for a proposal by the staff member.* You might say something like: "I notice in your guidelines that you have funded several affordable housing programs in our area. Our program helps homeless, unemployed women make the transition to employment by providing them with affordable housing and support services. Is this the sort of program that fits the foundation's guidelines?"
4. *Try to get a sense of the amount to ask for.* You should have already read through the list of grantees before you make the contact, to get a sense of the range of grants made by this funder. But ask the staff person for advice on this point. If he or she is hesitant to provide an answer, try throwing out some numbers to get a reaction. "I was just wondering what would be a reasonable amount for us to ask for."

Finding the Right Fit

When I first started fundraising, I liked the feeling of sending out a bunch of grant proposals. It really seemed as though I was getting something done then. Even if it appeared that there was only a re- mote possibility that the funder would be interested in our group, I'd send a proposal. After reading this chapter, you can probably guess that my strategy was not particularly effective. I've learned over the years that studying a prospective funder and narrowing your list to a small group of strong potential foundation and corporate supporters is a much more effective strategy. You may surface many potential funders and whittle your list down to just three or four that appear to be strong possibilities. That's OK. You'll be much more successful if you focus your efforts on funders that fit your organization and ministry.

Key Questions

1. What tools can you use to identify potential funders for your ministry?

_____

_____

_____

_____

2. What tools can you use to research potential funders for your ministry?

_____

_____

_____

_____

7

Building a Case for Your Ministry

"We filled in every part of the grant application, but still didn't receive the grant. What happened?"

When you write a grant proposal, you are not simply describing your organization. I'm always running into ministry leaders who think that they just need to write down all of the facts, and their grant proposal will be solid.

That's not all there is to it. Everything written in a grant proposal needs to be factual, but it also needs to persuade. You need to sharpen your content and language to show the funder why your group is worthy of consideration. You are building a case for both your program and your organization, and every part of the proposal needs to reinforce that case. Even the seemingly mundane parts of the proposal can help build the case for your ministry. For example, when describing the qualifications of staff members, don't just make a chronological list of work experiences. Shape the staff descriptions to focus on the qualifications most relevant to your particular work.

This chapter outlines how you can build a case for your ministry. These are preliminary steps to preparing your grant proposal. A case statement should be a series of sentences or an outline that is eventually expanded into a full grant proposal. Think of the case statement as a "pre-grant proposal," an opportunity for you to start writing down information about your ministry and sharpening it to make it persuasive.

Throughout the chapter, I use examples from a fictitious faith-based nonprofit group called We Can Kids Center to demonstrate the difference between simply listing facts about your ministry and building the case for it.

Your Niche

An important part of building a case for your ministry is identifying what makes your organization and program unique. In the geographic area where you work, there is probably no shortage of people who are doing good work, forming nonprofits, and launching programs. What makes yours special? What is your niche? As you work to build your case, consider how you're different from other groups in the following ways:

1. *The faith-based aspect.* Does the fact that you are doing faith-based work set you apart from other, similar organizations that are not faith-based? In what ways? Does the faith-based aspect have the potential to make your program more successful? If so, how?

2. *The unique aspects of the target audience you serve.* Are you working with a population that few other organizations serve? If so, whom? Are the people you are serving new to the area? Is the community just becoming aware of their needs? If so, what has brought these needs to your organization's attention?

3. *The program approaches you use.* Have you developed a new and innovative program approach? If so, what makes your approach innovative? Do you get program results that differ from those of similar organizations? What are those results?

4. *Your collaborative partners.* Are you drawing together a new group of partners in your ministry? What does the collaboration accomplish that a single organization couldn't?

5. *The skills and backgrounds of your staff and volunteers.* Are your staff members credentialed or experienced in special ways? How does that add to the quality of your programs?

Do you screen and train your volunteers differently from other organizations?

6. *The capacity of your organization.* Does your ministry have the capacity to launch and sustain the programs you are proposing? Where does your ministry have the strongest capacity? Where does your ministry need to build capacity?

The sections in the next few pages provide tools for you to make your case, building the parts of the case statement described in the list above.

The case for faith-based organizations

Too often, I run into faith-based organizations that seem embarrassed in the presence of secular funders, as though the faith aspect of their work were a liability. Instead, I think we need to consider why being faith-based is a reason to hold our heads up, why it strengthens our case rather than undermines it. Here are a few thoughts to help you make that case.

Congregations have built-in resources that other kinds of nonprofits may not. If your organization is a church or is partnered with churches, you probably have a built-in constituency of potential volunteers through the church, for example. Nationwide, one-third of all those who volunteer give their time within and for religious organizations, totaling 12 million hours of volunteer time annually.[1] Studies indicate that people who participate in a congregation are much more likely to volunteer, in part because opportunities to volunteer are presented to them on a regular basis and because community service has become the norm for many congregations. It's been my own experience, too, that it is easier to recruit a group of volunteers from within a congregation than from outside it.

Access to space in church buildings may be another plus for a faith-based organization. Church buildings may not be fully occupied or may not be used during the week, creating an opportunity for other groups to share office or program space. Space in a church may be free or at least less expensive than other types of space in your area. Also, church buildings often have features that other facilities do not. Where else can you find lots of meeting space, offices, an industrial kitchen, a gymnasium, and a performance space (the sanctuary—or, often, a large fellowship hall with a stage), all in the same facility? You won't find all of that in every church building, but in many you will, making it possible to pursue all kinds of programming that you couldn't do elsewhere.

And don't forget the financial base for your ministry that a church can provide, either through gifts from individual donors, through the church budget, or both. These types of gifts can leverage other kinds of support. When I worked for one church-based nonprofit, financial gifts from the members of the partner congregation helped leverage several large grants from local foundations. Church members gave gifts ranging from 50 cents to over $2,000, and all of these gifts indicated significant community support for our programs to local funders. This giving helped to sway grant decisions our way a number of times.

It's also good to remember that the resources available through faith communities can extend well beyond an individual congregation. Because your work is faith-based, you may be able to develop relationships with a whole network of partner churches, with their own people, money, and other resources to add to the mix. Your ministry may also be able to build relationships with local, regional, or national denominational offices, some of which have grant programs to support certain kinds of ministries.

Another advantage of faith-based organizations is that they may be more accessible to community residents than other types of nonprofits. For example, families in crisis may feel more comfortable approaching the church than a government agency or a secular nonprofit. Part of this comfort level with the church is that a pastor or other member of the church staff may be seen as more sympathetic than people outside the church. And churches often have a long-standing presence in the community that can make it seem the most familiar and safest place to go. Faith-based nonprofits that are not churches may enjoy these advantages as well. I have worked in several communities where ministry nonprofits developed trust with community residents much more readily than secular nonprofits, often because of the witness and commitment of the staff.

Ram A. Cnaan describes the American congregation as the primary provider of social services in this country and one of the last institutions that serves as the "glue" that draws people together. This role makes the local church a logical place for people to go when they need help. Cnaan explains:

> When someone is hungry and homeless, help is most likely to come from members of a local congregation. When children of working parents are left alone at home, the local congregation is most likely to offer an after-school latchkey program. Similarly, when people are discharged from alcohol rehabilitation centers, it is most likely that they will turn for support to the AA group housed in the local congregation. In other words, in America, congregations are the "hidden" safety net.[2]

Although the spiritual content of ministries can be controversial, it's also a selling point. More and more evidence points to the premise that some issues or problems are best dealt with using a faith-based approach. Even people outside the faith community are beginning to believe that God may be a key part of helping some people recover from addiction or illness, take responsibility for their families, and turn their lives around. Some research into faith-based health approaches, for example, shows a link between prayer and healing.

Some scholars have identified holistic ministry as more effective than government programs when a group is working with people who live in poverty and on welfare, precisely because ministry addresses the moral and spiritual issues as well as material needs.

Public-policy changes are not enough, because they can't bring about personal transformation. Holistic ministry, in contrast, addresses the emotional, physical, mental, and spiritual state of the whole person.

Another advantage of working with church congregations is the social capital they provide. Social capital, in this case, is the networks and relationships formed between people in the church, giving members connections to all sorts of resources like jobs, loans, housing, cars, day care, and counseling. In many churches, you can just put the word out about what you need, and someone will turn up who can help you or who knows someone who can. I've found that this social capital aspect of the church is particularly important for people who live in poverty. Poverty can be isolating, separating the people who live in it from the kind of networking relationships that would help them get needed resources. If your ministry focuses on children or adults who live in poverty, connecting them to the social capital of a congregation will only serve to enhance your program.

Another plus of faith-based approaches: they are often more successful in communities of color. For example, anyone who is serious about reaching out to African American or Latino people will probably need to work with the churches in those communities. Many communities of color don't separate the spiritual from other aspects of life as has historically been the case with European Americans. Many black churches, for example, are much more than a spiritual community. They are also the hub of social and family life, a place to get direction and advice on all aspects of life. Many health programs focused on the African American community work with churches, distributing health-prevention information and providing check-ups, with the goal of lowering the incidence of disease that disproportionately affects the black community.

The case for your target audience

In this part of the case statement, you identify the people your programs are for and build the case for that target audience. The first step here is fully describing your target audience. Ask yourself who they are (their demographic characteristics) and where they are (their geographic characteristics).

Your target audience is probably included in the mission and vision statements of your organization in some way, but the people in it may have some characteristics that you have missed. For example, your mission may be to "build assets among the youth of East St. Louis," but when you look at those you are serving, you realize that most of your programs are targeted to young African American women. That doesn't necessarily mean you have to change your mission statement, but the knowledge of whom you are actually serving can help you build the case for your target audience. Perhaps for your ministry the target audience is low-income seniors in your county, Protestant churches in the metro area, or recent immigrants from Asia.

Gathering statistics and other data about your target audience can also help you bolster your case. For example, census data may indicate some important facts about the people living in the geographic area you serve, such as their employment rate, their income level, and their ethnicity. A local academic institution or the United Way may have conducted a study on the people you work with and the issues you address, and a summary of that data may bolster your case statement. Data comparing your audience against people elsewhere in your state and the nation can be particularly useful. One organization I worked for focused on a neighborhood that had one of the highest teen pregnancy rates in the nation. We obtained that information from a local health clinic and the public-health department in our city. Keep your ears and eyes open for studies that are being conducted with your target audience and in areas where you work, and you may find something useful to include in your case statement. I've also found it helpful to get connected with the organizations that do this type of research—schools and universities, departments of local and state governments, and nonprofits dedicated to researching community issues.

After you have documented the demographic and geographic characteristics of your target audience, consider the following questions:

1. *What are the unmet needs of your target audience?* Describe, as fully as you can, the needs of your target audience. Needs might include things like "have limited access to health care," "need affordable housing," and "need training in how to mobilize volunteers." Documenting needs doesn't have to involve a full-scale research study. While published research and statistics can be useful to you, you can gather useful information just by talking informally with members of your intended audience.

   Your staff and volunteers also may have developed a "sense" about needs through the work they are doing. In my consulting work, I encourage staff of my client organizations just to start talking about what they are seeing and hearing in the community and from participants. It is often surprising how much knowledge is available internally in an organization. Without even looking at a research study, you may find out by talking to staff and volunteers that what seniors in your area really need is home health-care workers, or that the top concern of neighborhood residents is having a grocery store nearby.

Program participants are a great source of information on unmet needs as well. You may consider creating "feedback loops" within your programs, so that participants have a way to communicate on a regular basis the needs they are seeing and experiencing. I have seen groups gather this kind of feedback through program evaluation processes or through surveys or focus groups.

2. *Are there other organizations serving this same target audience?* Make yourself aware of other, similar groups working with the same target audience. Networking with your peers is a great way to find these organizations. If you are working in a particular geographic area, you might just want to drive around or walk up and down the street to see who else is out there. Knowing about the "competition" will help you understand what makes your organization different.

3. *If so, what makes our work different from theirs?* In the next few pages, I lay out how you might make the case for the uniqueness of your work—your program approaches, collaborative partners, unique qualifications of staff and volunteers, and the capacity of your organization.

The case for your program's approach

This is the "what" of your case statement—demonstrating what you plan to do to make an impact. Put down all of the facts about your program: the activities you will provide, where they will be held, how often, and when. It may be easiest to create a grid or a chart with headings like: "Program Activity," "Location," "Day of the Week," and "Time."

Facts about your target audience

We Can Kids Center serves youth ages 6 to 18 who live in the Sumner Hills neighborhood.

The case for your target audience

We Can Kids Center serves youth ages 6 to 18 who live in Sumner Hills. A majority of these youth live in poverty, and educational performance is a key issue for them. Sumner Hills high school students have the fourth-highest drop-out rate in the state.

Then consider why those elements of your program approach are important and unique. Do you use an approach that's new and different? Perhaps it's a brand-new curriculum, or an innovative approach that takes into account the special needs of immigrants. Maybe your uniqueness is the location where you offer your program and when it's offered. I'm aware of a faith-based AIDS ministry that sends outreach workers to places where the sex workers are, because that is a key group of people who need AIDS prevention and treatment resources. The outreach workers took the program to their new location; they go there in the middle of the night because that's when the potential participants are there. For that organization, it was a new where and a new when that helped build the case for its ministry.

Demonstrating your program results is another key aspect of building the case for your program approaches. You need strong program outcomes to attract funders. Or if your program is new, you need to set outcome goals for your program and demonstrate the strong promise of achieving them. A key part of setting outcomes is changing your mind-set. Instead of focusing just on the activities you will offer, start focusing on your customers and how their lives will be transformed. The time you invest in the development of program outcome goals is time well spent for your

Facts about your program's approach

The tutoring program at the We Can Kids Center teaches math and reading skills to fourth- through eighth-graders.

The case for your program's approach

The We Can Kids Center tutoring program is based on a structured academic curriculum that uses real-world examples and problem-solving to teach reading and math. The program has been used successfully with diverse groups of youth in other urban settings.

Two new program sites were opened last year at Redeemer Lutheran Church and Judson American Baptist Church. Both churches are located across the street from elementary schools, and the convenient sites draw youth into the program during after-school hours.

organization. It forces you to turn and look at what you are trying to accomplish.

The case for your collaborations

As mentioned previously, having the right collaborative partners can make the difference between a successful program and a marginal one. Hopefully, now that you are at the point of fundraising for your program, you've put some time and effort into developing collaborations with organizations that add value to the work you are doing. If so, you should "brag on" your partners. Build your case by demonstrating:

1. *The expertise your partners bring to the table, particularly if it complements or fills some gaps in your own expertise.* If you work with vulnerable populations, such as the homeless, chances are good that your organization is not set up to meet all of their needs. Being able to partner with groups that provide what you do not (health care,

housing, job training, jobs, for example) will serve to enhance the impact of what you do and will give your clients a greater chance of succeeding.

2. *Their connections to the community.* Your partners bring their networks with them, so be sure to count everyone they bring along as a part of what you have. Partners may work in different sectors from your group, bringing along government and corporate contacts that you don't have.

3. *The longevity of their work.* If you are a new organization (and even if you're not), partnering with a well-established group can bring credibility to your project. When I worked with several partner organizations to start a training program for pastors, we decided to partner with a well-known community organization that had an African American pastors' council that met monthly. Members of the council served as our first group of students. Our effort gained visibility and credibility through our partnership with this

---

Facts about your collaborations

We Can Kids Center collaborates with several neighborhood organizations: the Johnson Park Recreation Center, the Boys and Girls Club, and the Neighborhood Health Clinic.

The case for your collaborations

Our collaborative partners have helped us expand the number of youth we are serving and the types of programs that we offer. The Johnson Park Recreation Center worked with us to add girls' athletic programs at the center, including soccer and softball. The Boys and Girls Club added our location as a site for its leadership program, which provides opportunities for older youth at the center to do community service projects in the neighborhood. And the Neighborhood Health Clinic provides free health screenings and dental checkups several times a year for the youth who attend our center.

community group, helping to draw funding and additional participants to our new program.

4. *The concrete resources that partners bring to the effort, such as
staff, facilities, equipment, and vehicles.* Putting all of the partners'
resources together lowers the cost of doing business and is more
efficient than ownership by each partner of a building or van, for
example.

The case for your leadership and staff

Showing that the people in your organization are qualified is another important part of building the case for your ministry. The right
people (or the wrong ones) have a tremendous impact on whether
your organization and its programs will be successful. Your staff is a
critical part of this success, of course, but your board members and
other volunteers are key as well.

Putting together the right mix of people within your organization is critical, and promoting the mix you've achieved is part of
building your case. Successes in nonprofit life usually occur when a
great "smorgasbord" of gifts, skills, and experiences are drawn together. For example, most organizations need administrative types
and relational types—people who can run the front office *and* people who know how to counsel and help families in crisis. Depending
on what you are trying to do, you may need accountants, community activists, nonprofit directors, educators, corporate leaders,
parents, youth, clergy, and lawyers (to name just a few).

Demonstrating the qualifications of your staff is a critical part of
building your case. Of course, the experience and credentials of the
executive director should be highlighted, but don't forget about
your program staff members, who play a highly important role as
well. Larger organizations may want to include key administrators,
such as a chief operating officer or an associate director, to demonstrate that the organization has sufficient infrastructure to sustain
its programs.

Describing your board members and their qualifications will also
help to build the case for your organization. Be sure to list the professional qualifications of board members—their current jobs, their
educational backgrounds, and other boards on which they serve.
But don't forget to list the more informal and nontraditional expe-

Facts about leadership and staff

Joan Anderson earned her degree in child development from Kansas University and has an M.A. in child psychology from the University of Minnesota. She has been the executive director of the Children's Center of West Des Moines, Iowa, and Kids Network in St. Louis, Missouri; she now directs the We Can Kids Center.

The case for your leadership and staff

Joan Anderson has over 20 years of experience in child development and has successfully led three child-development organizations to expanded programs and financial success. She is seen as a national leader in the field, and is currently serving as the president of the National Child Development Association.

riences that board members often bring with them. You may have board members who are residents of the community you serve, for example, or they may be parents of youth in your program. Some of your board members may have informal volunteer experiences that are relevant to your work as well.

Finally, be sure to include your base of volunteers, another important human resource in your organization. It's not just staff members who "count." Particularly if you have a core of dedicated volunteers who help out in your programs on a consistent basis, be sure to include them as you build the case for your organization. A strong base of volunteers shows that you have broad community support. Volunteers are also cost-effective, bringing resources to people who need them for much less than a paid staff person would cost.

The case for your organizational capacity

You are also building a case for your organizational capacity—your group's ability to start, manage, and sustain your programs. All successful ministries start with great ideas. But it's the organizational capacity of your group that will bring great ideas to fruition and keep them around for a long time.

When building the case for your organizational capacity, consider whether you have the following characteristics:

1. *The human-resource capacity to attract and retain qualified staff.* Can you find the people you need to run your organization and its programs successfully? If so, do they stay around?

2. *The ability to raise the funds you need to sustain current programs and start new ones.* Are you ending the year in the black each year? Are you able to raise sufficient funds for most new program ideas that the organization agrees should be moved forward?

3. *The ability to plan effectively.* Does your organization have a strategic plan that identifies its vision, mission, key strategies, and values? Does your group have a good sense of what you are trying to accomplish in the next one to three years?

4. *A clear vision, mission, and focus.* Can you answer these questions about the work of your organization: who, what, where, when, how, and with whom?

5. *A board of directors that is governing the organization effectively.* Does your board understand its role? Are board members actively engaged in the life of the organization?

6. *Effective evaluation processes that help you gauge the impact of your programs and refine the programs to make them more effective.* Do you have desired outcomes for your programs and processes to measure them? Do you use evaluation data to improve the quality of your programs?

7. *Compliance with laws and regulations governing the nonprofit sector and processes to protect the organization from being successfully sued.* Do you file the legal papers you need to each year? Do you have proper insurance coverage to protect the organization and the people in it? Do you have volunteer and staff screening procedures?

Even if you believe that your organization has a great distance to go, there are probably at least some ways in which your group has moved forward organizationally during the past year. Focus on these accomplishments in your case statement, even if they are small, rather than thinking that you have to describe everything that's left to do to build your organization. I frequently work with executive directors who too readily talk about what their organization isn't, rather than what it is.

Another important aspect of organizational capacity is the willingness to continue to build capacity. If you have set aside the time and the money to train staff, develop your board, and hire consultants in such key areas as fundraising and strategic planning, use these facts to build your case too. Your willingness to identify weak spots and to strengthen them also reflects well on your organization. Organizations move forward more successfully when capacity building is always in the forefront.

Facts about organizational capacity

We Can Kids Center was founded in 1994 and has 15 staff members and 10 board members. Our funding comes from churches, foundations, and individuals, and the organization has three program sites.

The case for organizational capacity

In just the past year, We Can Kids Center has expanded its funding base by over 20 percent, attracting a number of new individual and foundation donors. In addition, the center created a new administrative director position and filled it with a qualified candidate with 15 years of experience in the field. The work of the new administrator is allowing our executive director to spend more of her time fundraising and developing new programs. Also, the strategic planning process we completed in the past year has helped to strengthen our board's involvement and to clarify the mission and vision of the organization.

Writing Your Case Statement

Use the following set of questions to write your own case statement. I have used "We Can Kids Center" as an example again, to give you a sense of what a case statement looks and sounds like. Again, always emphasize the unique aspects of your group, what sets you apart from other organizations doing similar work.

Rather than writing a full narrative in response to these questions, just sketch out an outline and a few phrases that will help you develop your full grant proposal later.

Whom does your organization serve?

- The We Can Kids Center serves youth ages 6 to 18 who live in the Sumner Hills neighborhood.
- High school students attending the neighborhood schools have the fourth-highest drop-out rate in the state.
- Most of our participants come from families that live in poverty.
- More than 200 young people participate every year.
- We have a special focus on girls, who have fewer programs available to them through other neighborhood agencies.

What programs and services do you provide?

- After-school tutoring—a structured program that uses a curriculum that, on average, has helped youth improve their reading and math skills by two grade levels in a year.
- College prep program—helps high school students improve their grades, select a college, and apply for admission.
- Arts programs—culturally specific programs, with a special focus on hip-hop.
- Leadership development—youth ages 14–18 are encouraged to use their vision and skills to serve the community. Done in collaboration with the Boys and Girls Club.
- Athletic programs for girls—soccer and softball offered in conjunction with the Johnson Park Recreation Center.

- Involvement of adult volunteers—100 adults volunteer their time at the center each week, serving as role models and a positive influence. The volunteers come from the network of 10 churches that worked together to develop the center in 1994 and continue to support it.

What are your program results?

- Seventy-five percent of the students in our college-prep program graduate from high school and enroll in college or technical school.
- Youth who participate in our tutoring program increase their reading and math skills by two grade levels, on average, every year they participate in the program.
- Through the leadership program, youth develop skills in budgeting, marketing, and fundraising.

Where do you provide programs?

- In Sumner Hills, particularly in the neighborhoods adjacent to Johnson Park. We have three program sites—the center itself and satellite programs at two nearby churches, Judson American Baptist Church and Lutheran Church of the Redeemer.
- The center is the only youth facility in the neighborhood.
- Characteristics of the community: while the Sumner Hills neighborhood was once home to some of the wealthiest families in the city, the area now struggles with a number of issues, including increasing crime, gang activity, and prostitution.

Who are your partners?

- A network of 10 partner churches that represents six denominations. Partner churches provide volunteers, supplies and funding for the center.
- The Boys and Girls Club offers its leadership program (serving 14- to 18-year-olds) on site at the Center.

- The Johnson Park Recreation Center provides softball and soccer programs for girls at our center.
- The Neighborhood Health Center provides free health and dental check-ups for center participants several times each year.

What is the capacity of your organization?

- A highly experienced executive director, who has successfully run two other youth development organizations.
- 250 committed and trained volunteers who help at the center each week.
- A growing financial base.
- An experienced and credentialed program staff, including three program directors with advanced degrees in social work.
- A history of successful programming—getting results with youth who have not succeeded in other types of programs.

Sing Your Own Praises

Being in the midst of launching and running a nonprofit organization can make it difficult to see what progress you're making. In my years as an executive director, I felt as though I was in the middle of a whirlwind, always being pulled and pushed by the immediate issues at hand. I remember being acutely aware of everything we weren't getting to—the programs we wanted to launch, the money we wanted to raise, the systems we needed to create. In this environment, it's difficult to take a step back and see all that you've accomplished.

Though it's difficult to sing your own praises, be sure to do it. Take the time and create the space to see how far you've come. For me, that's how writing a good case statement always starts. Make a list of your ministry's accomplishments, stick it to the wall, and keep adding to the list as you make progress. Always take time to review accomplishments at your staff and board meetings. However you do it, just be sure to keep those accomplishments in view and add them to your case statement.

Key Questions

How will your ministry build the case for:

1. Your faith-based approach?

   _____

   _____

   _____

   _____

2. Your target audience?

   _____

   _____

   _____

   _____

3. Your program's approach?

   _____

   _____

   _____

   _____

4. Your leadership and staff?

   _____

   _____

   _____

   _____

5. Your collaborative partners?

   _____

   _____

   _____

   _____

6. Your organizational capacity?

   _____

   _____

   _____

   _____

8

Writing a Winning Grant Proposal

Now, at last, you are ready to begin writing your grant proposal. When I taught grantwriting to my very first student, he kept asking, "When do I get to write? I thought you were going to teach me to write grant proposals!" We had spent weeks talking about the focus of his ministry, researching funders, and developing strategy, and he was getting impatient. What I said to him and what I will say to you is this: all of the work spent solidifying your focus and researching the funder up to this point will help you write a much more compelling, and ultimately successful, proposal.

Before You Begin

You'll need to know a few details about application forms and processes before you start writing the proposal.

Common grant application forms

It used to be that each foundation or corporate funder had its own application form and grant format. This diverse assortment drove grant writers crazy and caused nonprofit organizations to devote considerable time and resources to filling out all those different forms. Finally, a few years ago, funders in many states organized themselves and began to use a common grant application. Now each funder requests essentially the same type of information from

grant seekers, and you don't need to rewrite your proposal completely each time you submit it. However, I still strongly recommend that you tailor your proposal to the values and requirements
of each funder (as specified in the funder's written guidelines).
Making these changes will probably mean altering or adding just
several paragraphs, rather than rewriting the whole thing.

If a funder allows you to use the common grant application,
you will often find it on the funder's Web site or in the application
packet. If you don't find it there, the trade association for funders
in your state will have it as well. For example, in Minnesota, that
group is the Minnesota Council on Foundations; in Chicago, it's
the Donors Forum. To find the trade association for funders in your
area, look on the Giving Forum Web site at www.givingforum.org.
You can also type the phrase "common grant application" into your
Internet search engine with the name of your state and see what
pops up. You might also check with the United Way in your area or
with a nonprofit management-training program to get information
on the common grant application that is in use in your area.

The letter of inquiry

Some funders require you to submit a two- to four-page letter of inquiry before you turn in a full grant proposal. The thinking behind
this step is that you get the chance to run your idea by the funder
in a summarized form before putting all of the work into creating a
full-scale proposal. Some funders use an online process for this step,
requiring you to complete a questionnaire or submit a brief description of your idea through the funder's Web site.

Having to submit this letter first might seem an annoying additional step in the process, but it can provide you with valuable
feedback from the funder. If the funder says no after reading your
letter, you have just saved yourself some time that can now be spent
on more promising funding opportunities. If the funder says yes
and asks you to submit a full proposal, the yes will often come with
advice on what to "tweak" to improve your chances for funding.

The most important things about writing letters of inquiry are
to stay within the page limit specified by the funder and be concise.
The reason funders use a letter-of-inquiry process is so that they re-

ceive something brief from you first, something much shorter than a full grant proposal.

The length of a grant proposal

Most proposals to foundation and corporate funders will be from five to seven pages long, excluding attachments, such as the budget and your list of board members. There are exceptions, of course, so you will need to research each funder's guidelines to find out about page limits. If there are page limits, be sure to abide by them. If you exceed page-limit requirements, you run the risk that your proposal will be discarded without being read or that foundation staff will read part but not all of your proposal. One funder I interviewed had a three-page limit, and the office manager simply removed all additional pages from the proposals that came in with more than three pages.

Every funder I interviewed for this book emphasized that he or she preferred short grant proposals to long ones. Think of foundation staff receiving hundreds and hundreds (maybe thousands) of proposals in a year's time, and you can understand why funders prefer shorter proposals. When I first started writing grants, I wrote longer ones, thinking that the more information I included, the better the chance we would be funded. I have learned from personal experience that this is simply not the case.

The style of a proposal

I like to say that grant proposals should be written in a style that is both warm and professional. This is a business document, so be professional, both concise and to the point. It is also critical that you use correct grammar and avoid spelling and typographical errors. The spell-checking function on your computer is useful, but I still recommend that you have one or two people proofread the proposal before it goes out. Choose proofreaders who are strong writers and who are detail-oriented. They will catch errors, misspellings, and sentences that trail off into nowhere.

Once I sat on a grant-review committee that was considering proposals for educational programs for youth. You wouldn't believe the number of misspellings and grammatical errors in those proposals! We turned down the folk who didn't know how to write or spell, thinking that they would not be the best people to help youth improve their academic achievement.

I've emphasized being professional, but also be sure that your proposal has a warm tone. As ministry leaders, we are in the people business, and we should let our passion for people and their development shine through as we write grant proposals. Including stories about the people we serve is frequently appropriate, but be sure to protect the identities of your clients if you are revealing any personal details. You will also want to ask for permission to use those stories, perhaps developing a release form that will indicate in writing that people have given you their permission. Keep those forms in your file with the completed grant proposal.

When I teach grantwriting, I suggest that people write the proposal first with a strong focus on what the funder is asking for. Keep the funder's guidelines at your right hand as you write, and keep checking to make sure you are sticking closely to what is being asked for. Include all of that information, then take a step back and ask, "Am I telling our story?" It is possible to write a technically accurate proposal and leave out the warmth of your work entirely. You want to avoid this pitfall.

One ministry organization I headed had a successful reading program for youth from the neighborhood school. The program had bubbled up from schoolteachers in the community who were concerned that 30 to 40 percent of the children in each grade at the school were not reading at grade level. The funders always wanted to know about concrete results, so I wrote the first draft of my proposal focused almost entirely on the testing of students and the grade levels at which they were reading. This important information needed to be included in the proposal.

But when I took a step back and asked myself, "Am I telling our story?" I decided that the answer was no. Here is what I had left out: students in the program had become excited about reading. Before, reading had been discouraging for them, as they struggled with it and saw on a regular basis how they lagged behind other students in their class. The tutoring program had helped to lift their reading levels. Now, before the doors opened for our after-school program, a group of students gathered outside, pounding on the door and yelling, "Let us in! We want to read!" This exclamation became the heading for the opening paragraph of the grant proposal: "Let us in, we want to read!"

And there was more. The program had engaged more than 100 adult volunteers from several congregations who were going into these urban schools every week and working with youth. The relationships that developed through the program were meaningful to both the adults and children. Children had a caring, positive adult who was expressing interest in them. The adults were learning all about the challenges facing urban schools and their students. Many of these volunteers went back to their churches and their communities and shared these stories, recruiting more volunteers and securing other resources needed by the schools.

Your ministry has similar stories that you will want to be sure to include in your grant proposal.

Typical Content of a Grant Proposal

In the next several pages I've outlined the types of information that are usually included in a grant proposal. It is important, however, for you to review the guidelines for each funder to make sure you haven't left out any of the information requested. Also, it's not unusual for different types of grants to require different types of information. For example, what I've outlined here would be appropriate for a general operating or program grant, but a capital grant would likely include a description of the property to be purchased and the building to be built (see chapter 3).

What you are asking for

Tell the funder what you want right up front: how much money you want and what it will be used for. A complaint I hear often from program officers at foundations is, "I just want them to tell me what they want!" In the very beginning of the grant proposal (don't bury it on page 3), write in very clear terms:

1. *The amount of money you are asking for.* Researching the guidelines and the annual report from the funder should give you information on the amount to ask for. Look at the size of grants made to other, similar groups, and you'll at least get in the ballpark. Also, if you have a conversation with a foundation staff member, ask for advice on this. You do research so that you can avoid asking a $15,000 funder for $100,000—and vice versa.

2. *What the money will be used for.* Is it a program grant you want? Indicate that. Or perhaps you are looking for a general operating grant or capital gift. Be clear.

Background of your organization

Don't make this section of your proposal a boring recitation of your organization's history. Use it to "toot your horn" about how far you've come, the results you've achieved, and the impact you've made. Too often, I read grant proposals that include the driest possible description of the organization's history. I think, "If you aren't excited about what you've done so far, why should I be?"

Funders will read this section looking for your mission statement, your vision statement, and an overview of the programs you provide, so be sure to include those. This is also a place, though, to include the following:

1. *The passion of your founders and the reasons behind the founding of the organization.* Without describing all the details of your history, can you demonstrate the compelling reason for the organization to exist and the sacrifices made by those who formed the organization? For example, the impetus for our child-care center came from mothers in our community who wanted a safe and affordable place to take their children.

2. *Recent accomplishments.* Tell all about your successes in the past months and year, including the obstacles you've overcome. You want to show the funder how the organization has moved forward both programmatically and organizationally. You might include newly launched programs, bud-

get and funding growth, new staff and board members, and new collaborations and partnerships. If you've been working through a problem within your group, don't be afraid to describe progress on that as well. Example: "We ran a deficit last year when we lost a major government grant but have gained ground financially this year as we worked to expand our individual donor base and have secured several new grants."

Needs being addressed

You will also be asked to document the need or issue that your proposal is designed to address. How is it that your organization decided to move in this direction? Perhaps your group acted in response to the increased number of immigrants arriving from Africa, or statistics showing a need for health education. Maybe the number of school-age children in your community has grown, but the number of after-school programs has shrunk. Whatever the issue you are trying to address, the funder will want to see that you are knowledgeable about it and that someone else besides you thinks your program is meeting a need. Use the information at your disposal to demonstrate the facts about the situation.

Types of information that will help you demonstrate the needs include:

1. *Direct community feedback.* This is the best kind of information of all, since it shows that you took the time to talk with the people you would like to serve. You might decide to invite potential participants to a focus group to ask them what they really think, or conduct some individual interviews or surveys with key people. Another option would be to attend an event that members of your target group are participating in, just to listen. Apart from talking with individuals whose lives might be affected by your work, you may also decide to survey other organizations working in the same field, to get their thoughts on what you propose to do. These conversations could also lead to collaborative partnerships.

2. *Demographic data.* Census data can be an invaluable tool, particularly if your proposal focuses on a specific age group or ethnic group. For example, showing that 60 percent of all residents in the census tract where your youth center is located are under the age of 18 would bolster your request. New Web sites and computer software can help you break down census data in specific ways. The U.S. Census Bureau Web site (www.census.gov) is easy to navigate, even without the help of other software.

3. *Information from existing studies.* Colleges, universities, or research organizations in your area may have already studied the issue you are proposing to focus on. United Way and other philanthropic organizations frequently conduct this type of research as well. For example, you may find studies on school readiness, health disparities, small-business development, or services for immigrants. This is the type of information that would be hard to recreate on your own because of the expertise and time required. Media outlets frequently highlight major new studies, so you could become informed about studies useful to you just by keeping up with the newspaper or TV and radio news.

4. *Your own research, conducted in partnership with people or organizations with the needed expertise.* If you are relatively sure that the need you are proposing to address has not yet been studied by anyone else, you might consider partnering with people or institutions in your area to get the research done. Colleges and universities frequently require their students to complete original research, so, for example, you may find free help from local students who can conduct surveys or review and compile statistics.

You may also be able to convince a local school or research nonprofit that studying this need is important, and that institution can raise money and complete the project. This approach to gathering data will take longer, of course, than using existing information or surveying your participants. So if you are looking for information to include in a grant proposal that is due in the near future, you will need to use one of the other approaches outlined here.

One note of caution: it can be easy to pack your proposal with so much negative information about needs that it may appear that you think very little of the people you are attempting to serve. For instance, if you are working on the East Side and all you've written about the East Side in your proposal is how run-down and crime-ridden it is, funders may wonder what your commitment to the community really is. Balance information about needs with information about community assets such as schools, parks, churches, and people who are working to better the community.

Program plan and timeline

If you are requesting funding for a program, the program plan and timeline are the "meat" of your proposal. Funders will read this section to see if you have really thought through what it will mean to implement your program. You might imagine that funders are asking as they read: "Sure, you have a great idea, but can you pull it off?"

How you planned the program. Document in a paragraph or two the planning process for your program. One of the best ways to plan a program, and one that is appealing to funders, is to gather a group of stakeholders to discuss the issues and design the program. For example, if you are proposing an initiative to reduce youth crime, you might consider inviting the following categories of people to the table: law-enforcement officials, parents, youth, staff from other youth-serving agencies and local public schools, clergy, and people working in the county social-service system.

Funders particularly like to see involvement of potential program participants in the planning. For example, for your proposed youth crime initiative, did you invite any youth to the table? One group I worked for was convinced that what teenagers in the community really wanted was more basketball programs. However, when group leaders asked the kids, they said they wanted jobs and job training. If group members hadn't had a conversation with potential participants, that group could have invested resources in a program that wasn't really needed or wanted.

Planning a program by involving a number of stakeholders can take more time, but in my experience, that approach produces much more effective and longer-lasting programs. Involving a number of stakeholders can help you work on complex community problems more effectively, since you'll get different perspectives and can invite people with a variety of skills and expertise into the process. When using a planning process that involves a number of stakeholders, I would recommend that you appoint or hire a facilitator to work with you, to keep your process focused, and to manage disagreements that may arise.

Program Goals. Start your program section with a brief description or list of the primary goals of your program. These goals should have a direct relationship to the program outcomes that are described in the evaluation plan for your proposal (see page 154). Program goals should identify your target audience and what you hope that your program activities achieve. Some sample program goals:

- High school students from our community will succeed in school.
- Heart disease among African American women will be reduced.
- The Smith Avenue commercial strip will be revitalized.

My recommendation would be that each of your programs have no more than three goals. Depending on what you are proposing to do, you might feel good about having just one or two goals. For me it has always been a temptation to list many goals, so that it appears that the program has more impact. Realistically, though, the more focused you are on just a few goals (or even just one), the more successful your program will be. You'll be devoting all of your program resources and the weight of the organization to a focused approach.

Activities you propose to carry out. Put down in writing, in as specific terms as possible, all of the activities that are a part of your program. I find sometimes that organizations leave pieces out of this section, giving the funder an incomplete picture of the program itself. Of course, the activities you describe should have a direct tie to your program goals.

Make this part of your narrative engaging, drawing a word picture for the funder of what exactly happens in your program. I always include enough details in this section so that the funder can visualize what participants see and engage in. Ask yourself: "When a participant walks through the door of our program, what will she see, what will she have a chance to be a part of?" For example, your job-training participants will be involved in skill assessment, job-training classes, computer training, resume development, mentoring, job interviews, job placement, and job support groups. Whew! That's a lot of programming, but if your group provides it all, you should document it in this section.

I should also note that if you work in collaboration with other groups to provide a spectrum of programming, be sure to include information on the services that participants receive from your collaborative partners. Also include in this section the number of people you expect to be served by each program activity and who will be organizing and leading the activity. One more tip: using lists, bullet points, or tables can be helpful, providing a quick visual aid for the funder of the scope of your program.

Timeline. Tell the funder when you will implement the program. At what time of year will it begin? How many days a week will you be offering it and for how long each time? Also, be sure to factor preparation time and follow-up into your program timeline. For example, work for your after-school program won't begin on the day the kids come through the door for the first session of the program. There will have been many months of the following kinds of activities, all done in preparation for the launch of your program:

- talking with community members about the program.
- establishing collaborative partnerships with other organizations.
- identifying a location for the program.
- recruiting staff and volunteers.

- purchasing supplies and equipment.
- recruiting youth for the program.

And once you have launched your program, there will be follow-up activities, including program evaluation and revision of the program.

Funders will want to see in your timeline that you understand everything that's involved in launching your program, from start to finish. Don't leave out some steps because you think foundation staff will be more impressed with you if you move more quickly. If anything, the opposite will happen. Funders often say to me that they are concerned about groups that have unrealistic expectations about how long it takes to implement a program. They would rather see a realistic plan from you than a pumped-up one with a timeline that is too ambitious.

Evaluation plan

"What will change in the world as a result of your work?" I believe this is arguably the most important question you must answer in your proposal. Funders are tired of hearing only about needs. They want to see concrete results, or at least the strong promise of achieving them. So when you put together your proposal, don't describe just the poverty and violence in your community. You will need to identify, in specific terms, how your organization will respond to these issues and what will be the result. What will happen to the participants in your program? Will they:

- decrease their involvement in criminal activity?
- improve their school attendance?
- participate in community-service activities?
- set positive goals for the future?

If you develop a results orientation early on, your organization and its programs will be much more successful in addition to having an increased chance of getting funding. You may want to consider hiring an evaluation consultant to help you develop evaluation tools, or to do an evaluation of your programs, or both. Program evaluation is a field unto itself these days, and I have found the advice and input of evaluation consultants to be invaluable. It has become typical to include the cost of evaluation in the program budget of a grant proposal.

Funders usually request that you include in your proposal a couple of paragraphs on your evaluation plan, which would include the proposed outcomes of your programs and the tools you will use to measure whether you've achieved those outcomes. Desired program outcomes could include items such as these:

- 50 percent of participants secure living-wage jobs and keep them for one year or more.
- 50 percent of participating students graduate from high school.
- A majority of students improve their reading skills by two grade levels or more over the course of a year.

Look at the chart on page 156 for more ideas on how to translate your list of program activities into program outcomes.

Measurement tools gather both quantitative and qualitative data that demonstrate whether you've achieved your intended results. Some tools measure more short-term outcomes (usually six months to one year), and others measure longer-term outcomes over a period of years. One challenge of measuring long-term outcomes is that participants may disappear off your "radar screen" by moving or changing jobs. To truly measure long-term outcomes, you will have to develop a long-term strategy for staying in touch with your participants. Possible measuring tools include:

- Pre-test and post-test of participants.
- Focus groups with participants, preferably conducted by a neutral third party, perhaps an evaluation consultant hired for this purpose.
- Surveys of people who work with participants, such as staff, teachers, or volunteers, noting the changes they have noticed.
- A review of statistics concerning participants, such as how many get jobs and keep them for how long or how many graduate from high school.

Sample Program Outcomes and Measurements for an Evaluation Plan

Not outcome-focused

Offered three tutoring sessions per week during the school year, serving 200 children

Program provided housing for 5 families

Three hundred youth went to camp

Twenty-five youth helped build a home for a family in the neighborhood

The Credit Union provided loans to 30 businesses

Outcome-focused

Tutoring students improved their reading skills by an average of 2 grade levels, as measured by a reading skills inventory test

Program helped 5 families stabilize their lives, as demonstrated by consistent employment over a 6-month period and staying off alcohol and illegal drugs

Youth developed self-sufficiency skills at camp, through a "survival skills program," as measured by their ability to plan a camping trip, work with others, and respond to the challenges of camping in the wilderness.

Twenty-five youth worked together to build a home, developing skills in planning, cooperation and carpentry. Half of these youth went on to jobs in the skilled trades.

The Credit Union provided loans to 30 businesses:

- that were turned down for loans elsewhere
- that generated 300 jobs in urban communities as a result of the loans
- 75% of these jobs went to unemployed workers

Collaborations/partnerships

Almost all foundation and corporate funders now see collaboration as a necessary prerequisite to receiving funding. Foundation and corporate staff won't be impressed with your "we're going to save the world all by ourselves" attitude. Instead, they will be looking for the ways that you maximize relationships with other organizations so that your participants will best be served.

It used to be that funders would be satisfied if your group was only loosely connected to other organizations. Just referring participants back and forth, for example, would have been enough. But times have changed, and now funders focus more on authentic and deep collaborative relationships that might be characterized by the following:

1. *Shared planning processes that include a diversity of people and organizations.* In my experience, funders aren't inclined to fund initiatives that have been developed by one group, with others invited to participate only later. Make your planning processes authentic, and work hard to include a diversity of people from the very beginning. This approach takes longer and can be more frustrating, but it almost always leads to more effective programs and is better for the community in the long-run.

2. *Shared space.* The program you develop through your planning process may be offered at several locations that are owned by several different organizations. Or several programs may be located in one place. Sharing space is one way to save money (potentially), but another real benefit is the synergy that can develop between staff and programs when everyone is in one location. More opportunities arise to share ideas and "work out the kinks" in a program.

3. *Shared staff.* Some organizations opt to share staff as a way to collaborate, having one staff person work on multiple programs or at multiple sites. This is a tricky type of collaboration to implement, since you want to avoid pulling one staff person in too many directions. Identify one supervisor for the staff involved, and set out a clear schedule

for each staff member who is shared, identifying what he or she is to work on, and with whom, during different parts of the week.

4. *Shared funding.* You might decide to apply for funding as a group, dividing both the expenses for the initiative and any grants that are received. It is not uncommon in this situation to designate a "fiscal agent"—one organization within the group that will receive funds and disburse them, typically for a fee. Also, when sharing funding, you will want to spell out in specific terms who is responsible for which activities and how much those activities will cost. Work to avoid conflict after you get the grant over who gets how much money by agreeing on the specifics during your planning process.

5. *Shared expertise.* No one group knows everything, so it's in your best interest to find partners who can fill in the gaps where you need knowledge and expertise. Funders love to see such partnerships and understand that a synergy can develop between groups that can substantially increase the impact of programming. For example, if your organization provides job training to unemployed women, you may also find that those women need child care and mental-health services, two fields in which your group has little expertise. Partnering with a child-care organization and a mental-health clinic would make sense, as those organizations can help remove obstacles to employment for your clients. Everyone benefits when these kinds of partnerships happen successfully.

6. *Shared supplies and equipment.* Buying supplies or equipment in bulk for several organizations can result in cost savings. Or perhaps certain pieces of equipment can be shared between groups in a collaborative arrangement—computers, a vehicle, or athletic equipment, for example. Just be sure to create a schedule of who gets to use which equipment and at what times.

Funding plan or list of other funders

Funders will typically ask you to attach a list of your current funders. They will be most interested in other corporate and foundation donors, but don't forget to include other types of support as well, from churches, service groups like Kiwanis or the Lions Club, and individual donors (include only a total for all individuals, not everyone's name). Corporate and foundation staff will look at your funder list to:

1. *Determine if any "gatekeeper" funders have signed on to support your group.* In every community there are corporations and foundations that serve as leaders in the philanthropic community. Get them to support you, and other funders will follow suit. Sometimes these are the largest foundations; sometimes they are the ones known to have a rigorous review process.

2. *Determine whether you are doing the hard work of fundraising.* Funders don't like to support groups that aren't exploring a number of funding options. For example, asking a foundation for a $50,000 grant when the budget for your program is $50,000 is a grant-seeking faux pas. In my 20 years of fundraising, I have encountered very few funders that want to foot the whole bill for a program or organization. Demonstrate in your funder list that you are aware of other funding options and are exploring them.

Putting together a funder list or funding plan can be intimidating when you are just starting out as an organization. Initially, your list will probably be pretty short. This is acceptable, as long as you alert the funder to the fact that your organization is new. Be sure to include all of the support you've received so far, including a total of individual donations, church support, and gifts from community groups and service clubs. Also, you may want to highlight in-kind gifts such as the donation of office space, supplies and equipment, or even volunteer time, if you are primarily a volunteer organization. Even if the total you have raised so far seems small to you, demonstrating to funders that you have been working hard to secure resources will be meaningful to them.

Management capabilities/biographies of staff members

Funders typically want to see short biographies of the management staff, to see if the people actually running the organization have relevant qualifications. Include a bio for the executive director, and also for the program director who oversees the program for which you are seeking funds. You may also include a short bio of the board chair if that person's qualifications will bolster your request.

Bios usually include work experience and educational background but may also focus on relevant volunteer or community experience. For example, your executive director may not have a degree in nonprofit management from the local university, but if she has lived in the community you are serving for years and has volunteered extensively in programs for seniors (the focus of your agency), be sure to include both of those facts about her in her bio.

Grant Attachments

Most funders will require you to attach additional information to your grant narrative, providing them with a look at your organizational structure, funding, and finances. Be sure to read this list of attachments carefully and include all of them with the proposal. If you forget any of the attachments, your proposal may be ineligible for consideration by the funder. I've listed below the grant attachments that foundations and corporations typically require.

IRS determination letter

This letter is the document from the IRS that indicates your organization is a nonprofit, tax-exempt, 501(c)3 organization. Most funders now require that their grantees be 501(c)3 nonprofits. I have encountered a few funders over the years that were willing to fund groups of grassroots individuals without nonprofit status, but these have been few and far between.

If you are in the process of applying for your federal nonprofit status, ask the funder if you may use a fiscal agent to receive grants on your behalf while you are waiting for the IRS to respond to your federal application. A fiscal agent is another nonprofit that will receive and disburse funds on your behalf, usually for a small fee.

A list of board members and their primary affiliations

Funders will want to know more about the people who govern your organization before they make a grant. They will look at board members' professional affiliations (their "day jobs") but will also be interested in other types of experiences board members have, including boards they serve on, other ways they volunteer in the community, or expertise they have developed over the years.

Also, more and more funders are interested in community representation on boards. That is, they want to know whether the people being served by the organization are participating in its governance. For example, funders may look for ethnic diversity on a board if the community served is diverse. They may also watch for client representation. For example, if your group provides job training to the unemployed, is there an unemployed person on your board to lend his or her perspective to organizational decision making?

Budgets

A budget is one of the most important parts of a grant proposal, but I've found that many groups spend too little time preparing them—and funders notice. I actually start here when writing grant proposals. Preparing a budget forces you to think through all aspects of your proposed project, including the staffing and activities. Starting with your budget is a way to cut to the chase quickly.

Funders frequently request two kinds of budgets—a program budget and an organizational budget. If you are requesting program funding, prepare a separate program budget that details all of the anticipated expenses. Funders like to see a level of detail in program budgets that grant seekers frequently leave out. For example, don't just include a line item called "staff" with $100,000 attached to it. Spell out what the staff positions are ("youth worker," "administrative assistant") and detail the salary and benefits costs for each position. A sample program budget is outlined on page 162.

When preparing your program budget, be aware of the cost of the program per participant. To get this number, divide annual cost of the program by the number of participants served per year.

Sample Program Budget for Youth Tutoring Program

This is a sample of a program budget for a youth tutoring program, identifying all of the expenses for the program in a year's time. If your ministry has a tutoring program, it may have expenses that are much larger or much smaller than those included in this budget, depending on the scope of your work.

Annual Expenses

Salaries	**$44,000**
Program Director (1 FTE)	$30,000
Outreach Worker (.5 FTE)	$12,000
Percentage of Office Manager's time devoted to program (10%)	$2,000
Benefits	**$8,500**
Health insurance (full-time staff)	$3,500
Dental (full-time staff)	$800
Payroll Taxes (10% of salaries—percentage varies)	$4,200
Staff Training	**$2,000**
Program Supplies	**$4,000**
Reading and math curriculum	$1,000
Books for students	$500
Food ($50/wk)	$2,500
Liability Insurance (20% of organization's overall expense)	**$2,000**
Rent (use of 25% of the facility)	**$12,000**
Transportation (bus rental for 5 field trips)	**$1,500**
Field Trip Fees	**$1,200**
Volunteer Recognition	**$800**
Student Incentives/Awards	**$800**
Printing	**$500**
Postage	**$500**
TOTAL PROGRAM EXPENSE BUDGET:	**$77,800**

There are no rules of thumb on how much a program should cost, but be aware of this number in case the funder has questions. If your cost per participant is relatively high (perhaps thousands of dollars annually), you'll need to be able to demonstrate why that level of expenditure is necessary. Perhaps you are working with a particularly vulnerable population that needs many types of services, or you are working in a concentrated way with a small group of people to achieve higher impact.

You will also need to submit a budget for your entire organization with each grant proposal you send out (see the next page for organizational expense budget categories). Funders like to see a breakdown of the costs for each program as well as administrative expenses for the organization. The rule of thumb used by most funders is that administrative expenses for an organization should not exceed 25 percent of its annual budget.

An administrative expense is any money spent that is not focused strictly on implementing programs. Fundraising expenses are always considered administrative, and accounting/financial-management expenses are usually in that category as well. Many organizations allocate staff costs by figuring how much time each individual (even the executive director and administrative staff members) spends implementing a particular program. You can also allocate other expenses to your program expense budgets, including portions of your liability insurance, printing, postage, and facility expenses. Talk with your accountant or bookkeeper to get some help on allocating expenses to the proper budgets.

Financial reports

Funders like to make grants to groups that are financially stable and are able to account for their funds. You can understand why. It is risky at best to fund groups that are running huge deficits or that don't have systems for tracking donations or expenditures. For this reason, funders typically request a monthly or quarterly financial statement from grant seekers. It is likely you will be asked for the following financial reports:

1. *A balance sheet* (also known as a statement of financial position) provides a snapshot of the financial health of your ministry at one moment in time, showing both assets and liabilities.

Organizational Budget Expense Categories

These are typically the types of expenses you will need to include in an annual budget for your organization. Depending on the focus of your ministry, you may need to add other expense categories as well.

Salaries

All wages paid to program and administrative staff. Includes full-time, part-time, and temporary employees.

Benefits

All employee benefits paid for by the organization, including health, dental, and life insurance; retirement benefits; and any other benefits; also payroll taxes, including FICA/Medicare, state unemployment, and worker's compensation.

Staff development

Staff training and education. Expenses associated with attending conferences and classes, for example, or bringing consultants in to lead a session on-site.

Contractors

All fees paid to people who perform services for the organization who are not employees. The IRS has a strict definition for who can be considered an employee and who cannot. Check this definition before you put someone in the "contractor" category.

Facility expenses

Cost of renting or owning office and program space. Include rental fees or mortgage payments and utility costs.

Program supplies

Expendable supplies needed for specific programs, including items like food, craft supplies, and curriculum.

Office supplies

Pencils, paper, staplers and staples, paper clips, and other supplies used in the office.

Telephone

Cost of local and long-distance service, cell phones, and other equipment costs.

Equipment

Purchase or lease of nonexpendable items needed for the operation of programs or the organization. Computers are typically included in this category, as is furniture.

Travel

Mileage and parking reimbursement for staff; also cost of air fare, car rental, and other expenses associated with nonlocal travel.

Printing

Cost of hiring a company to print materials such as brochures, newsletters, and annual reports; also expenses related to having a copier on site.

Postage

Stamps, bulk-mailing fees, and courier services, such as UPS and FedEx.

Liability insurance

Books, subscriptions, and memberships

Purchase of books and magazine subscriptions related to the organization's work; membership in professional associations and other groups.

2. *A statement of activity* (or income statement) shows the expenses incurred and the income received by your organization over a set period of time, typically a month, a quarter, or a year.

3. *A statement of functional expenses* shows expenses broken down by functional area (administration or fundraising, for example) or by program (transitional housing or day care).

Even if your organization is small, I recommend that you get professional help preparing your financial statements. Doing so will help you avoid costly mistakes and will also provide a level of accountability and objectivity that funders like to see.

Most smaller nonprofits do not need to hire a full-time accountant. Some accountants work on a contract basis. Technical-assistance organizations in your area may provide accounting services to smaller nonprofits for a nominal fee. One organization I worked for used an accountant from the local technical-assistance organization, and the cost was only $200 per month.

Financial audit

Most corporate and foundation funders will also require you to have completed an audit of your organization's finances before they will consider your proposal. An audit takes place annually and provides a check of your financial totals and a review of financial processes and procedures within your organization. If you are an organization that has an annual budget of less than $300,000, you are not legally required to complete an audit. However, if you are serious about seeking grant funding, you will need to spend the time and money to get this important financial review completed. If you are a brand-new organization and haven't completed your first fiscal year yet, talk with the funder to see if submitting a current financial report will suffice.

If you have never conducted an audit before, you'll need to find an auditor, preferably a certified public accountant who has experience auditing nonprofit organizations. The best source of referrals is other nonprofits that have hired the auditor and been happy with his or her work. Ask around, and you'll probably find someone who will meet your needs.

Involvement of corporate volunteers in your organization

Corporate funders usually like to see that their employees are involved with an organization before they will consider making a grant. It will be important for you to be aware of the affiliations of board members and other volunteers, so you can tap into these corporate connections as you are seeking funds. Identify your corporate volunteers in a separate attachment or include their names in one of the first few paragraphs of your proposal narrative.

Putting It Together

One of the values of writing a grant proposal is getting all of the aspects of your ministry—the stories, programs, finances, and people—into one document. Just the act of putting it all together is an accomplishment and frequently brings more order and clarity to a ministry. Many ministry leaders I have worked with have described the grantwriting process as difficult but good, as it forced them to ask key questions and get at some aspects of their ministries that had not been developed. When you complete your proposal, just know that you have accomplished something significant, even before you submit it to any funders.

Key Questions

1. Look back through the chapter at the elements of a grant proposal. Which parts of a grant proposal is your ministry group prepared to write?

    _____

    _____

    _____

    _____

2. Which parts of a proposal do you need to do more preparation on before you begin to write?

_____

_____

_____

_____

3. What aspects of your ministry story do you need to be sure to tell in your proposal?

_____

_____

_____

_____

4. Which grant attachments do you have already?

_____

_____

_____

_____

5. Which ones will you need to secure?

_____

_____

_____

_____

9

Following Up with the Funder

Well, you finally got the grant proposal out the door after much preparation and hard work. Now what do you do? Do you: (a) Pace the floor and bite your nails? (b) Call the funder every day to see if there is news? (c) Keep working on fundraising? (d) Pray a lot? (e) Yell at the foundation staff if you don't get funded? (f) Both c and d?

In my experience, there are few things that are as hard as waiting for news of the grant proposal you've just submitted. You put your heart and soul into it, and now you are at the mercy of the funder. You may feel as though the funder's decision-making is taking forever, as though everything hinges on this decision, as though there must be something else you can do to get a yes.

My most productive waiting times have been spent in prayer and focused on continuing the process of fundraising (both c and d). Keep reminding yourself that fundraising is an ongoing process and an everyday effort. Although the grant proposal you just sent in may be an important one, it is certainly not the end of your fundraising story, regardless of the outcome. You will get an answer about your proposal eventually. This chapter is designed to help you know what to do while you are waiting and once you've received an answer.

What Can I Expect?

What happens next after you submit your grant proposal? There will be a waiting period before you get your final answer from the funder. Sometimes the funder will ask to visit your ministry to gather more information about your organization and its work.

How long does it take?

Most proposal review processes take anywhere from two to six months. In my experience, the average is about three months. It's important to keep this timing in mind if you have immediate financial needs for something; grants usually aren't an immediate answer. I've seen some grant review processes that move more quickly, if the foundation has a review committee or board that meets frequently. Some foundations authorize staff members to approve grants below a certain amount dollar amount, avoiding a lengthy grant review process that involves a board or committee.

Ask the funder when you submit your proposal when it will be reviewed and when you'll be notified of a decision. Then write the date in your calendar so you won't have to keep calling to find out about the status of your grant. Usually a funder will notify you of the decision in a letter, often enclosing a check if the answer is yes.

It is considered appropriate to call a funder after you know that your proposal has been reviewed to ask whether it has been approved. In my experience, most foundation staff will give you that information over the phone, but I still encounter a few who won't, who prefer to notify applicants in writing.

What are my chances?

What are the chances that your proposal will be funded? Your chances of getting a yes will vary by funder and the type of program or organization for which you are seeking a grant. I don't think there is a rule of thumb about what percentage of proposals are typically funded, because there are so many factors that influence funding decisions. However, I usually assume when I send out grant proposals that I will get a yes about one-third of the time. So it is important to explore a number of funding options and prospective grants, knowing that not all of the proposals you send out will be approved.

Typically, corporations and foundations will fund only a fraction of the proposals they receive. Sometimes a funder will say no the first time you submit a proposal, but your potential for getting a grant may increase as the funder becomes more aware of your organization and the results of your programs. Follow the steps below to receive feedback on your proposal and to develop a relationship with the funder, and the answer may be yes next time.

The site visit

Some foundation and corporate funders will conduct a site visit with you after you have submitted your grant proposal to gather more information about your organization and your request. Site visits are initiated by the funder and are part of the proposal review process. These are different from other visits the funder may make, perhaps at your invitation. Being asked for a site visit does *not* mean that you will receive a grant. It simply means that the funder is interested enough to look more closely at your group.

Site visits are a way for a funder to get a visual conception of what you are doing, to get a close-up sense for the "feel" of your organization and its programs. It's also an opportunity for you to "strut your stuff"—show your passion, demonstrate your programs in action, highlight the competence of your staff and volunteers. In my experience, site visits can be a time when you can really "clinch it," convincing the funder that the grant should be yours. Funders typically send one or two staff members on a site visit. Some funders hire consultants to conduct these visits instead of sending staff. The consultants are usually people who have expertise in the fields in which potential grantees are working. The foundation staff I interviewed expressed some strong do's and don'ts for site visits. Some tips from them (and from me):

1. *Decide what you want to communicate at the site visit and then make sure you say it.* Maybe you have some more good news since you submitted the proposal—more grant funding came through, for example, or you saw some new program successes. Sometimes when I write a grant proposal,

I think of a few more details I want to add after I send it off. This is the "frosting" you have an opportunity to add during a site visit.

2. *Don't have too many people from your organization at the site visit.* The funders I know said they prefer to have the person in charge of the program, one board member, and the head of the organization at the meeting, and probably no one else. One foundation staff member I interviewed said: "I'm just not interested in a dog-and-pony show at a site visit. Don't have 20 people there, all in their Sunday best. I want to talk to the core people who are most involved in implementing programs." Another foundation staffer said that one organization she reviewed had 10 people in attendance at the site visit: "We had to yell across the table to talk to each other!"

3. *Choose carefully which people will attend the site visit with you.* When choosing a board member to attend, or if you have a choice of program staff, focus on people who are articulate and can add something important to the conversation. You may also want to think about choosing people who will complement each other—perhaps putting a quieter "numbers person" together with a more exuberant program person. My style is more sedate and linear, so I tend to choose people to be in site visits with me who are full of stories and outgoing enough to tell them.

4. *Don't be too formal.* The funder won't be expecting a formal presentation from you—they already have that on paper. Mostly I heard from foundation staff members that they like to be informal, chat about the program, and get to know you better. One funder said, "At the site visit, I don't want to feel like I am the FBI or the IRS, coming to do an investigation. I just want to talk person-to-person. We both care about the community, and we have that in common. I want to hear your story from the heart, why you care, how you got involved, and how the organization has evolved."

5. *Make sure you have a copy of your grant proposal and its attachments handy.* The funder may refer to specific parts of the proposal, and you'll want to have it right in front of you so you that can answer questions quickly.

If You Get a No

Getting a no is hard, but if you are serious about getting grant funding, being turned down will always be part of the experience. Seeking grants is a competitive business, and usually funders say no to half or more of the groups that submit grants. Sometimes many more than half of the proposals are rejected.

Your "no" will probably come in a letter in the mail that says something like this: "The Firstcorp Foundation thanks you for submitting a proposal for our consideration. Unfortunately we will be unable to provide funding at this time. This is in no way a reflection on the fine work that you do in the community. Our resources are simply too limited to fund all of the worthwhile projects. Good luck to you in your endeavors." It is standard for corporations and foundations to send form letters, without specifying why your proposal was turned down, so don't be discouraged by the reply.

Here is my best advice for the times when the funder says no. First, don't take it personally. Because you have put so much effort and heart into your organization and the grant proposal, it will be hard not to take a no personally. But funding decisions are not a statement on your character, your competence, or the worth of your organization. Most often, funders will need to say no simply because they didn't have enough money to fund all of the worthy requests they have received. The more you can see that it's really not personal, the easier fundraising will become for you.

Second, follow up with the funder. All the funders I interviewed for this book said they were open to organizations calling them to discuss why they received a no. *Of course,* if you are angry, wait until you have calmed down to call. Then ask the foundation staff member if he can give you any feedback on why your request was turned down. You should expect to have a short conversation, possibly just five or ten minutes, but don't be surprised if the funder says that the decision was purely financial—the foundation just didn't have enough money to fund all of the worthy requests.

The value for you in these conversations is that you can get honest feedback on your proposal that will help you improve it. You might learn for example, that your program outcomes weren't clear enough, or that you hadn't demonstrated the need adequately, or

that the funder was wondering about your lack of collaborative relationships. Comments like this are like gold to you, providing insight into how you can improve your chances of getting funded.

You may also get some positive feedback during one of these
calls. You may find out, for instance, that 10 proposals were funded
and yours was number 11. You came so close! Or staff people may
tell you that they really liked your model or your staff members or
your community connections. Comments like these are also valuable
to you, because now you know what to emphasize in your funding
requests. Make sure to document the funder's comments—whether
positive or negative—in a file with other documents related to that
funder (everything you sent them and everything they sent you).

If you believe that the funder is a good fit for your ministry, ask
a staff member to visit. A tour of your programs will give the funder
a better sense of your organization and may increase your chances
of getting funded the next time you apply. One of my ministry clients suggested this approach to me, stating that she has had success
with this strategy: "I find that a visit after a 'no' is a great time to
get to know the funder and see if we could have a chance to apply
again. I did that with one funder this year and it turned into a 'yes'
the next time around. 'No' from a funder might just mean 'No, we
don't know your organization well enough yet.'"

If You Get a Yes

Getting a yes is what we all hope is the outcome of our grant-
seeking process. You may find out when the funder sends you a letter in the mail with a check. Or the funder may tell you by giving
you a call after the decision has been made. The yes may seem to be
the end of the process, because you've achieved your goal of getting
a grant. However, the yes is just the beginning of your relationship
with the funder, one that could continue over the long term if you
cultivate it through communication and recognition.

Keep in mind that a yes may mean that you receive only part
of the funding you requested. Organizations frequently receive a

grant that is smaller than the one requested, and you will need to decide how to handle that situation. Given this reality, it's a good idea to seek funding from a number of sources, not just one or two. One caution: be careful about moving forward with projects before you have secured all of the funding for them. I have watched groups move forward with half the money they needed when their grant requests were not fully funded. This decision can set your organization up for failure, hurting the community you are trying to serve and damaging your reputation with funders. It is better to take the time to raise the money you need, communicating with funders that do say yes to your proposal that you need a little more time to meet your fundraising goals.

After you get a yes, you need to follow up in several ways:

1. *Identify one person in your ministry who is the point person for communication with the funder.* In smaller organizations, this is typically the executive director, and for larger groups, it is often the development director. This doesn't mean that your point person is the only one in your ministry who will ever talk to or see the funder, but this person will coordinate communication, so that a number of people from your group aren't all talking with the funder at the same time about the same things. Also, identifying one person makes it more likely that these important follow-up and relationship-building tasks will occur. Otherwise, they might fall off the agenda in the busy life of your ministry.

2. *Send a thank-you letter immediately, no matter how you find out that you have been approved for a grant.* Preferably, send a brief letter that is personalized for that particular funder. If someone has put in a good word for your organization with the funder (a corporate employee, for example), let that person know about the grant as well, and encourage her to send a thank-you letter, too. In addition to your letter, you can send a short e-mail expressing your thanks to the program officer you have been working with. I am always surprised to hear from foundation staff about how many organizations do not follow through on the simple and

important step of saying thank you. One funder recently said to me: "I don't make grants to his group any more, because he never says thank you!"

3. *Acknowledge the funder.* It's appropriate to acknowledge funders in your written material, particularly if they have made gifts above a certain amount (you'll decide that amount within your organization). List funders in your annual report, for example, and include them in a list in your newsletter. If a funder sponsors a particular program, it might be appropriate to include its name on the program brochure or flyer. For example: "This program is made possible in part by a gift from the Johnson Family Foundation."

Major capital grants are often made with the expectation that a building, or part of it, will be named for the donor. These are usually formal agreements put together by the funder and the development staff of an organization.

Staying in Touch with the Funder

You should communicate periodically with the funder to keep the program officer or other decision-makers updated on your progress. You'll need to strike a balance between communicating much too frequently and not frequently enough. With larger foundations and corporations, you are working to stay in touch with foundation staff members who may have hundreds of organizations they are responsible for. Think about this point before you add these folk to your list for the weekly e-mail update (what I'm saying is, "don't do it"!). I've found that a good approach with these larger funders is to attend meetings or conferences where you know they'll be. You can bump into them and have a short chat, keeping them up to date on what's happening with your ministry, or even ask about a proposal you are thinking about sending to them. But be sure to keep your conversation short; don't monopolize someone's time at a public event.

In contrast to the way the larger foundations operate, the staff or family members running smaller foundations may use a much more hands-on approach in working with their grantees and may like to receive more frequent communication from you. I had a funder who made grants through her small family foundation who liked to fund just a few organizations so that she could be much more involved with each grantee. In our case, she had expertise that was valuable to us, and she helped plan our program and advised us on implementing it. She enjoyed getting regular e-mails about how the program was developing. If you have funders like this who are highly engaged with your organization, you could invite them for coffee or lunch periodically to give them a more regular, personalized update.

I received a wide variety of responses from the foundation staff members I interviewed about how they like to stay in touch with their grantees. From what they told me, I would recommend that you do the following:

1. *Always complete your required reports.* Some funders will require you to file periodic reports, providing them with information on how your project is coming. In my experience, a report is usually required annually, but some funders ask for them more frequently. Keep in mind that you will need to complete the required reports before you can ask the funder for another gift. Typically, funders will provide you with the questions you will need to answer in your report, but if they don't, expect that your report will need to contain the following information:

   - a restatement of your proposed outcomes and objectives.
   - progress made on those outcomes and objectives.
   - successes achieved during the grant period.
   - lessons learned during the grant period.
   - any changes made in the proposed program or project.
   - a financial report on how the funds were used.

2. *Communicate with your corporate and foundation funders two to four times a year.* That should be sufficient. The exception would be smaller foundations that are interested in being more hands-on, as described above.

3. *Always invite funders to significant events in the life of your organization.* The ribbon-cutting for the new facility would fall into this category, as would the launch event for a major new program. You can probably think of some other major events in your organization to which you would want to invite your financial supporters.

4. *Make opportunities for funders to see your programs in action.* For example, if the Smith Foundation sponsored your arts program, be sure to invite the foundation staff members over at a time when they can see the students painting, acting, and dancing. In my experience, giving funders a live picture of where their money went is worth 10,000 words on paper. And if they get a chance to see what the program looks like now, funders often have thoughts and dreams about what the program could become in the future and how their money could help it to get there. Usually, the executive director of an organization will host a meeting or event like this, and key program staff members will be present as well.

5. *Send your newsletter and annual report to funders that support your group.* Not everyone reads these, but I've had a fair number of foundation staff who say that they do. One funder told me recently that she and her staff read these carefully, passing them around the office and discussing them in staff meetings (though I think this practice is probably the exception). Send your written materials to the one or two people on a foundation staff with whom you work most closely, not to everyone and their brother and their brother's secretary.

Reporting Program Changes or Bad News to a Funder

Sometimes, despite our best efforts and a well-thought-out plan, our proposed program or project doesn't turn out quite as we expected. Maybe your collaboration with the schools falls apart, or you lose your star staff person and can't launch the program on schedule. When you develop a program plan and budget and begin to implement them, something will inevitably be different from what you expected.

If that's the case for you, you need to be honest with your funders about the changed situation. It's preferable to communicate major program changes or difficulties when they occur. Don't wait until your annual report is due. In my experience, most funders understand that program changes or "bumps in the road" are typical and are willing to work with grantees who are honest with them.

I would recommend making a phone call to your foundation contact to discuss the matter, and be prepared with some solutions to the problems you've encountered. For example, don't just call and say: "We're three months behind on the construction of the new building, and we don't know what to do!" Instead, call and say something like: "We're three months behind on construction, but we should still be able to launch the program on time, because the local community center across the street has agreed to let us use some space temporarily."

You will want to avoid surprising the funder. And of course, you need to avoid deception for a number of reasons, not least because foundations are usually well connected in the community, and funders will probably find out about the difficulties you've encountered even if you don't tell them. Also, as people of faith we need to be Christlike—honest and forthright—in our business dealings.

Funders are typically flexible with their grantees on unanticipated changes and delays. However, it's possible that a funder may ask you to return a grant or to reallocate it if things have not gone as planned. You can certainly try to negotiate with funders in these situations, making alternative suggestions to what they propose. Ultimately, though, you need to respect the funder's wishes, to be ethical and to maintain your reputation in the funding community.

A Continuous Cycle of Building Relationships

When you've worked long and hard on a grant proposal, it's easy to look at it as the one thing that will make or break your fundraising efforts or your ministry. In reality, fundraising is a continuous cycle of building relationships. In my experience, it's an every-week-of-the-year activity, and no matter how hard you work, there will always be some funders who say "yes," some who say "no," and others who say "maybe." As you begin or expand your fundraising program through grant-seeking, stay focused on the bigger picture of building relationships over a period of time, rather than on the answer you get to a single grant proposal. It's sticking with it over the long term that will strengthen your ministry.

Key Questions

1. How will you prepare for a site visit with a funder?

   _____

   _____

   _____

   _____

2. If your grant proposal is funded, what will your next steps be?

   _____

   _____

   _____

   _____

3. If your grant proposal is not funded, what will your next steps be?

   _____

   _____

   _____

   _____

4. How will you stay in touch with funders that provide support?

   _____

   _____

   _____

   _____

Appendix A

Common Grant Application

Many foundations and corporations use a common grant application that is also used by the other funders in the state or region. Below is the common grant application used by many foundations and corporations in Minnesota. You can find the common grant application used in your area through your local council on foundations or other funder group. See www.givingforum.org for members of the Forum of Regional Associations of Grantmakers. *The application form that follows is reprinted with the kind permission of the Minnesota Council on Foundations, Minneapolis, Minnesota*

Minnesota Common Grant Application Form

Revised December 2000

Dear Nonprofit Colleague,

We are pleased to introduce an updated version of the Minnesota Common Grant Application form. Minnesota grantmakers developed this form to make the grantseeking process simpler and more efficient for nonprofits. For ease of use and to eliminate unnecessary duplication of work, you may reproduce any part of the form you find helpful including the COVER SHEET and BUDGET forms.

Keep in mind that every grantmaker has different guidelines and priorities, as well as different deadlines and timetables. Before submitting this application to a potential funder, it is very important that you check to see whether your project or program matches their published interests. Any funder that has agreed to accept this form may request additional information as needed.

STRATEGIES FOR SUCCESSFUL GRANTSEEKING

1. **Do your research** to determine whether the foundations' and corporations' goals and objectives for grantmaking are consistent with your type of grant request.
2. After you do the research, find out the preferred method of contact for the grantmaker, and

contact the grantmaker to secure their specific grantmaking guidelines. Many grantmakers generally like to have initial contact with you before receiving a written proposal.

3. Include a cover letter with each proposal that introduces your organization and your proposal, and makes a strategic link between your proposal and the funder's mission and grantmaking interests.

4. Type and single-space all proposals.
5. Answer all the questions in the order listed.
6. Submit the number of copies each grantmaker requests according to their guidelines.
7. Do not include any materials other than those specifically requested at this time.

RESOURCES

- Call, write or check the Website of each grantmaker to obtain a copy of their funding guidelines (for a list of Minnesota grantmaker sites, visit MCF's Web site at www.mcf.org; select "Links of Interest").

- Use MCF's *Guide to Minnesota Grantmakers* and other directories listing foundations' interests and processes.

- Visit a Foundation Center Collection Library in Minneapolis, St. Paul, Fargo, Duluth, Rochester or Marshall-SW State.

For a list of grantmakers that accept the Minnesota Common Grant Application Form, or to download the Form, visit MCF's Web site at:
www.mcf.org/mcf/grant/applicat.htm

Minnesota Common Grant Application Form

Grant Application Cover Sheet

You may reproduce this form on your computer

Date of application: _____   Application submitted to: _____

Organization Information

Name of organization _____   _Legal name, if different_ _____

Address _____   _City, State, Zip_ _____   _Employer Identification Number (EIN)_ _____

Phone _____   _Fax_ _____   _Web site_ _____

Name of top paid staff _____   _Title_ _____   _Phone_ _____   _E-mail_ _____

Name of contact person regarding this application _____   _Title_ _____   _Phone_ _____   _E-mail_ _____

Is your organization an IRS 501(c)(3) not-for-profit?   ____ Yes   ____ No

_If no_, is your organization a public agency/unit of government?   ____ Yes   ____ No

_If no_, check with funder for details on using fiscal agents, and list name and address of fiscal agent:

_____   _____   _Fiscal agent's EIN number_ _____

184

Proposal Information

Please give a 2-3 sentence summary of request:

Population served: Geographic area served:

Funds are being requested for (check one) *Note.: Please be sure funder provides the type of support you are requesting.*

_____ General operating support   _____ Start-up costs   _____ Capital
_____ Project/program support   _____ Technical assistance   _____ Other (list) _____

Project dates (if applicable): _____   Fiscal year end: _____

Budget

Dollar amount requested: $ _____

Total annual organization budget: $ _____

Total project budget (for support other than general operating): $ _____

Authorization

Name and title of top paid staff or board chair: _____

Signature _____

185

Minnesota Common Grant Application Form

PROPOSAL NARRATIVE

Please use the following outline as a guide to your proposal narrative. Most grantmakers prefer up to five pages, excluding attachments, but *be sure to ask each individual funder if they have page limitations or any additional requirements.* Also, include a cover letter with your application that introduces your organization and proposal and makes the link between your proposal and the mission of the grantmaker to whom you are applying. For assistance with terms, refer to MCF's Web site (www.mcf.org; select "Grantseeking in Minnesota").

I. ORGANIZATION INFORMATION

A. Brief summary of organization history, including the date your organization was established.

B. Brief summary of organization mission and goals.

C. Brief description of organization's current programs or activities, including any service statistics and strengths or accomplishments. Please highlight new or different activities, if any, for your organization.

D. Your organization's relationship with other organizations working with similar missions. What is your organization's role relative to these organizations?

E. Number of board members, full-time paid staff, part-time paid staff and volunteers.

F. Additional organization information required by each individual funder.

II. PURPOSE OF GRANT

General operating proposals: Complete Section A below and move to Part III - Evaluation.
All other proposal types: Complete Section B below and move to Part III - Evaluation.

A. General Operating Proposals

1. The opportunity, challenges, issues or need currently facing your organization.
2. Overall goal(s) of the organization for the funding period.
3. Objectives or ways in which you will meet the goal(s).
4. Activities and who will carry out these activities.
5. Time frame in which this will take place.
6. Long-term funding strategies.
7. Additional information regarding general operating proposals required by each individual funder.

B. All Other Proposal Types

1. Situation
   a. The opportunity, challenges, issues or need and the community that your proposal addresses.
   b. How that focus was determined and who was involved in that decision-making process.
2. Activities
   a. Overall goal(s) regarding the situation described above.
   b. Objectives or ways in which you will meet the goal(s).
   c. Specific activities for which you seek funding.
   d. Who will carry out those activities.
   e. Time frame in which this will take place.
   f. How the proposed activities will benefit the community in which they will occur, being as clear as you can about the impact you expect to have.
   g. Long-term funding strategies (if applicable) for sustaining this effort.

Minnesota Common Grant Application Form

III. EVALUATION

A. Please describe your criteria for success. What do you want to happen as a result of your activities? You may find it helpful to describe both immediate and long-term effects.

B. How will you measure these changes?

C. Who will be involved in evaluating this work (staff, board, constituents, community, consultants)?

D. What will you do with your evaluation results?

ATTACHMENTS

Generally the following attachments are required:

1. Finances (*for assistance with terms, check MCF's Web site at www.mcf.org.*)

   • Most recent financial statement from most recently completed year, audited if available, showing actual expenses. This information should include a balance sheet, a statement of activities (or statement of income and expenses) and functional expenses. Some funders require your most recent Form 990 tax return.

   • Organization budget for current year, including income and expenses.

   • Project Budget, including income and expenses (if not a general operating proposal).

   • Additional funders. List names of corporations and foundations from which you are requesting funds, with dollar amounts, indicating which sources are committed or pending.

2. List of board members and their affiliations.
3. Brief description of key staff, including qualifications relevant to the specific request.
4. A copy of your current IRS determination letter (or your fiscal agent's) indicating tax-exempt 501(c)(3) status.
5. If applying to a corporate funder only: if an employee of this corporation is involved with your organization, list names and involvement.

Be sure to check each funder's guidelines, and use discretion when sending additional attachments.

PROPOSAL CHECKLIST

- ☐ Cover letter.
- ☐ Cover sheet.
- ☐ Proposal narrative.
- ☐ Organization budget.
- ☐ Project budget (if not general operating grant).
- ☐ Financial statements, preferably audited, showing actual expenses including:
  - ☐ Balance sheet.
  - ☐ Statement of activities (income and expenses).
  - ☐ Statement of functional expenses.
- ☐ List of additional funders.
- ☐ List of board members and their affiliations.
- ☐ Brief description of key staff.
- ☐ IRS determination letter.
- ☐ Confirmation letter of fiscal agent (if required).
- ☐ Additional information required by each individual funder.

189

Minnesota Common Grant Application Form

ORGANIZATION BUDGET

This format is optional and can serve as a guide to budgeting. If you already prepare an organization budget that contains this information, please feel free to submit it in its original form. Feel free to attach a budget narrative explaining your numbers if necessary.

INCOME

Source

Support

	Amount
Government grants	$
Foundations	$
Corporations	$
United Way or other federated campaigns	$
Individual contributions	$
Fundraising events and products	$
Membership income	$
In-kind support	$
Investment income	$

Revenue

Government contracts	$
Earned income	$
Other (specify)	$

$ _____

$ _____

Total Income $ _____

EXPENSES

Item	Amount
Salaries and wages	$ _____
Insurance, benefits and other related taxes	$ _____
Consultants and professional fees	$ _____
Travel	$ _____
Equipment	$ _____
Supplies	$ _____
Printing and copying	$ _____
Telephone and fax	$ _____
Postage and delivery	$ _____
Rent and utilities	$ _____
In-kind expenses	$ _____
Depreciation	$ _____
Other (specify)	$ _____

Total Expense $ _____

Difference (Income less Expense) $ _____

Minnesota Common Grant Application Form

PROJECT BUDGET

This format is optional and can serve as a guide to budgeting. If you already prepare project budgets that contain this information, please feel free to submit them in their original forms. Feel free to attach a budget narrative explaining your numbers if necessary.

INCOME

Source	**Amount**
Support	
Government grants	$
Foundations	$
Corporations	$
United Way or other federated campaigns	$
Individual contributions	$
Fundraising events and products	$
Membership income	$
In-kind support	$
Investment income	$
Revenue	
Government contracts	$
Earned income	$
Other (specify)	$
	$
Total Income	$

EXPENSES

Item	Amount	%FT/PT
Salaries and wages (breakdown by individual position and indicate full- or part-time.)	$	
	$	
	$	
	$	
	$	
SUBTOTAL	$	
Insurance, benefits and other related taxes	$	
Consultants and professional fees	$	
Travel	$	
Equipment	$	
Supplies	$	
Printing and copying	$	
Telephone and fax	$	
Postage and delivery	$	
Rent and utilities	$	
In-kind expenses	$	
Depreciation	$	
Other (specify)	$	
Total Expense	$	
Difference (Income less Expense)	$	

193

Appendix B
Typologies of Faith-Based Programs and Organizations

The Working Group on Human Needs and Faith-Based and Community Initiatives is a project of Search for Common Ground, an organization working to transform the way people deal with conflict. The working group put together a report of 29 recommendations "to increase the capacity and effectiveness of community and faith-based organizations in meeting human needs" (Working Group on Human Needs and Faith-Based and Community Initiatives, *Finding Common Ground: 29 Recommendations of the Working Group on Human Needs and Faith-Based and Community Initiatives* [Washington, D.C.: Search for Common Ground, 2002], 3.) To read the full report, go to www.sfcg.org and search for "29 recommendations." The report includes two charts. Typology 1 summarizes "faith characteristics of social service and educational organizations," identifying the characteristics of five types of faith-based organizations. Typology 2 identifies the faith characteristics of the programs supported by the five types of faith-based groups.

The group was initiated by former U.S. senator Harris Wofford and former U.S. Senator Rick Santorum, with the goal of seeking "common ground on appropriate ways of increasing the opportunities for people in need to get help from community-based organizations, including those inspired by religious faith." The 33-member working group, composed of stakeholders in the civic sector with a diversity of views, met for seven months.

The excerpts from the 29 recommendations that follow are reprinted with the kind permission of Search for Common Ground, Washington, D.C.

Table 1:
Typology
of faith
characteristics
of social service
and educational
organizations

	Faith-saturated	Faith-centered
Mission statement	Explicitly religious	Explicitly religious
Founding	By religious group or for religious purpose	By religious group or for religious purpose
Controlling board	Explicitly religious. May be a) self-perpetuating board with explicit religious criteria; b) board elected by a religious body	Explicitly religious. May be a) self-perpetuating board with explicit religious criteria; b) board elected by a religious body
Selection of senior management	Faith commitment an explicit prerequisite	Faith commitment under-stood to be a prerequisite
Selection of other staff	Religious faith is very important at all levels; and most staff share	Religious faith is very important for faith-centered projects, but is sometimes

	organization's faith commitments		less important in other positions. Most staff share founders' faith commitments
If affiliated with an external agency, is that agency religious?	Yes		Yes
Financial support	Overwhelming majority, if not all, from private (often) religious sources		Substantially private; explicit policy of refusing funds that would undermine above policies (1.-5.)
Receives reimbursement for entitlement benefits (e.g., food stamps Medicaid/Medicare, child care)	Often, but encounters different conditions among different programs, levels of government, and administrators		Often, but not automatic; may encounter rejection or resistance based on program content
Would requiring a separate 501(c)(3) be considered problematic?	Yes for some, no for others		Usually not

Faith-related	Faith background	Faith-secular partnership	Secular
May be either explicit or implicit	Implicit (e.g. general reference to "promoting values")	No reference to religion in mission of the partnership or the secular partner	No spiritual content, but implicit or explicit to references values often present
By religious group or for religious purpose	May or may not be founded by religious group	No reference to spiritual views of founder	No reference to spiritual views of founder
Some board members may be required or expected to have a particular faith or ecclesiastical commitment but not all	Board might have been explicitly religious at one time, but is now inter-faith; very little concern for faith commitment of board	Program controlled by secular partners, with heavy input from faith partners	No discussion of faith commitment of board members
Normally (perhaps by unwritten expectation) share the founders' faith	Not relevant whether they share the faith commitment of founders	Required to have respect for, but not to share partners' faith	Consideration of faith commitment considered improper
Project staff expected to have knowledge, sensitivity to faith commitment of founders;	Almost no attention to whether any staff share a faith commitment; religious beliefs may	Staff expected to understand and respect faith of partners; program relies significantly on	No consideration of faith commitment of any staff

religious beliefs motivate some staff/volunteers	motivate some staff/volunteers	volunteers from faith-based organizations	
Often	Sometimes	Sometimes	No
Funding is a mix of religious and secular sources (private and/or government)	Majority of funding is from secular sources (private and/or government)	Major funding from secular sources; in-kind contributions of space and time from faith-partners	No attention to religious commitment of donors; virtually all funding is from secular sources.
Usually	Always	Always	Always
Almost never	Almost never	Not for secular partner, yes if faith-based partners were required to do so	Never

Table 2: Typology Faith characteristics of programs/projects

	Faith-saturated	Faith-centered
Religious content of program	Explicit, extensive mandatory religious content integrated throughout the program; staff and clients are expected to engage in religious activities	Explicit religious content that is usually integrated with social service provision, but not to the degree that clients cannot opt out of explicitly religious activities. May be segregated into separate components (e.g., when mandated by government funding.) Staff are explicit about their faith commitments but respect the option of non-participation
Main form of integration of religious content	Integrated/mandatory	Integrated/optional, or invitational

200

with other program components		
Expected connection between religious content and outcome	Expectation of religious change and belief that such change is essential to desired outcome (e.g., drug rehab)	Strong hope for religious change and belief that such change significantly contributes to desired outcome
Religious environment (building, name, religious symbols)	Usually	Usually

201

Faith-related	Faith background	Faith-secular partnership	Secular
Very little religious program content and entirely optional; clients may be invited to participate in religious activities outside program parameters, or hold informal conversations with staff. The religious component is seen primarily in the act of caring for the needy rather than involving participants in religious activities	No explicit religious content in program. Religious materials or resources may be available to clients who seek it out. The religious component is seen primarily in the act of caring for the needy rather than involving clients in religious activities	No explicit reference to religious content	No reference to religious content; exclusive use of medical and social sciences
Invitational or relational	Passive	Relational or passive depending on	None

		depending on volunteers/staff	No expectation of religious change
Little expectation that religious change or activity is necessary for desired outcome, though it may be valued for its own sake	No expectation that religious change is needed for desired outcome	Religious change is not necessary for outcomes, but it is expected that the faith of volunteers from religious partners will add value to the program	
Often	Sometimes	Sometimes program may take place in secular or religious environment	No

Notes

Chapter 1

1. Thomas H. Jeavons and Rebekah Burch Basinger, *Growing Givers' Hearts: Treating Fundraising as a Ministry* (San Francisco: Jossey-Bass, 1995), 95.

Chapter 3

1. Jane Ferguson, "Corporate Philanthropy: Giving Derives from Role of Business in Society," *Giving Forum* 29, no. 2 (Spring 2006): 1.

2. Donors Forum of Chicago, "Glossary of Terms in Philanthropy," http://www.donorsforum.org/resource/grant.d.glossary.html.

Chapter 5

1. Working Group on Human Needs and Faith-Based and Community Initiatives, *Finding Common Ground: 29 Recommendations of the Working Group on Human Needs and Faith-Based and Community Initiatives.* (Washington, D.C.: Search for Common Ground, 2002), 3. The organization's Web site is www.sfcg.org.

2. Ram A. Cnaan, *The Invisible Caring Hand: American Congregations and the Provision of Welfare* (New York and London: New York University Press, 2002), 284.

3. Ronald J. Sider, Philip N. Olson, and Heidi Rolland Unruh, *Churches That Make a Difference* (Grand Rapids: Baker Books, 2002), 12.

Chapter 6

1. Joyce Foundation, "Education Guidelines," www.joycefdn
.org/GrantList/Guidelines.aspx (accessed Nov. 27, 2006).
2. Lilly Endowment, Inc., "Religion," www.lillyendowment
.org/religion.html (accessed Nov. 27, 2006).
3. Ibid.
4. General Mills, "General Mills Foundation Grant Application Guidelines," www.generalmills.com/corporate/commitment/
grants_application.pdf (accessed Nov. 27, 2006).
5. Sheltering Arms Foundation, "The Sheltering Arms Foundation Grant Guidelines," www.sheltering-arms.org/
grantguidelines2007.pdf (accessed Nov. 27, 2006).
6. Mustard Seed Foundation. "Granting Priorities," www
.msfdn.org/grants/index.cfm?fuseaction=grants (accessed Nov.
27, 2006).

Chapter 7

1. Cnaan, *Invisible Caring Hand,* 213
2. Ibid., 281.

Bibliography

I have included a few texts and Web sites here on writing grant proposals, but also a number on other ministry and management topics such as strategic planning, community ministry development, and research into the effectiveness of faith-based approaches. As you prepare to write your grant proposal, you'll likely find that you need to work on a number of issues within your organization, including evaluation processes, planning, and board effectiveness.

Books

Barry, Bryan W. *Strategic Planning Workbook for Nonprofit Organizations,* revised and updated. St Paul, MN: Amherst H. Wilder Foundation, 1997.
> This book provides a five-step process for completing a strategic plan for your nonprofit group, covering preparation steps, a situation analysis, and the writing and implementation of the plan.

Cahalan, Kathleen A. *Projects That Matter: Successful Planning and Evaluation for Religious Organizations.* Herndon, VA: Alban Institute, 2003.
> A book for project leaders and teams about basic project planning and evaluation. It introduces readers to the five basic elements of project design and describes a six-step process for designing and implementing a project evaluation and for disseminating evaluation findings.

Calhoun, John. *Philanthropy and Faith: An Introduction.* Washington, D.C.: National Crime Prevention Council, 2003.

This booklet does a great job of describing the relationships that develop between faith-based organizations and foundation and corporate funders. A typology of faith-based groups is offered, and a number of examples of faith-philanthropy partnerships are listed. You can view this material or download it at the Web site of Faith and Service Technical Information Network (FASTEN) at www.fastennetwork.org

Carlson, Mim. *Winning Grants: Step by Step,* 2nd edition. San Francisco: John Wiley & Sons, 2002.

Solid, practical advice on all of the steps involved in writing a grant proposal. I like the section on how to develop program ideas fully *before* asking for money—a step that too many groups skip over in the rush to get the money.

Cnaan, Ram A. *The Invisible Caring Hand: American Congregations and the Provision of Welfare.* New York and London: New York University Press, 2002.

A fascinating study of how and why American congregations get involved in community service, and the resulting impact on the community.

Dudley, Carl S. *Community Ministry: New Challenges, Proven Steps to Faith-based Initiatives.* Herndon, VA: Alban Institute, 2002.

An updated version of a classic text that outlines, step by step, how churches can engage in community ministry. Dudley describes the steps to understanding the community and your congregation and provides advice on getting organized and forming an organization. Each chapter includes numerous examples of congregations and their experiences with community ministry.

Hummel, Joan M. *Starting and Running a Nonprofit Organization.* Minneapolis: University of Minnesota Press, 2000.

A user-friendly guide to getting your nonprofit organization up and running. This book is heavy on the budgeting and financial-management pieces, and the chapter "Managing Financial Outcomes: Budgeting the $$$" has an easy-to-follow process for developing a budget, including budget worksheets.

Jeavons, Thomas H., and Rebekah Burch Basinger. *Growing Givers' Hearts: Treating Fundraising as Ministry*. San Francisco: Jossey-Bass, 2000.

This book focuses on developing a spiritual mind-set for fundraising: fundraisers are ministers, and the primary goal of fundraising is helping donors develop generous hearts. Sections include "Six Essential Characteristics of Fundraising as a Ministry," "A Brief History of Christian Fundraising," and "What the Bible Says about Giving and Asking."

W. K. Kellogg Foundation. *Evaluation Handbook*. Battle Creek, MI: W. K. Kellogg Foundation, 1998.

If you need to begin the process of program evaluation in your ministry, check out this booklet, available for download at the W.K. Kellogg Foundation Web site (www.wkkf.org). It includes a section on program/project evaluation that is particularly useful. I found the section on data collection methods (pp. 70–87) especially helpful.

———. *Logic Model Development Guide*. Battle Creek, MI: W. K. Kellogg Foundation, 2004.

Logic models are one way to develop an evaluation system for your ministry. A logic model plots out flow charts showing the target audience, assumptions, process, outcomes, and impact. This isn't my favorite way of working on program evaluation (it makes my head hurt!), but many people like it, and you may encounter some funders who require you to develop a logic model. This booklet is available for download at the W.K. Kellogg Foundation Web site (www.wkkf.org), and is a comprehensive guide to logic models, including concrete examples from a community clinic.

Klein, Kim. *Ask and You Shall Receive: A Fundraising Training Program for Religious Organizations and Projects,* participant manual and leader manual. San Francisco: Jossey-Bass, 2000.

Kim Klein is a guru of grassroots fundraising, and these books (participant and leader manuals) translate her fundraising approach into a training program specifically for faith-based groups. The books are structured as a training series to be taught to a group; they cover the following topics: the case statement, the role of volunteers, direct mail, special events, major gifts, and telephone solicitation.

Queen, Edward L. II, ed. *Serving Those in Need: A Handbook for Managing Faith-Based Human Services Organizations.* San Francisco: John Wiley & Sons, 2001.

This anthology addresses management issues for faith-based nonprofits, focusing on community development programs in particular. The three chapters on fundraising provide practical advice on developing an overall fundraising program and seeking funds from both government and foundation sources.

Sherman, Amy L. *Reinvigorating Faith in Communities.* Fishers, IN: Hudson Institute Publications, 2002.

Makes a case for the many ways that faith-based organizations contribute to community transformation, citing examples and research. Chapter 2, "How Congregations Serve Communities," provides a bibliography of research into the effectiveness of faith-based programs.

————. *Restorers of Hope: Reaching the Poor in Your Community with Church-Based Ministries that Work.* Wheaton, IL: Crossway Books, 1997.

Restorers of Hope makes the case for faith-based, relational ministry, citing many examples of successful ministries from around the country. The book is filled with practical advice on how to get a community ministry off the ground, including sections on collaboration and designing a relational ministry.

Sider, Ronald J., Philip N. Olson, and Heidi Rolland Unruh. *Churches That Make a Difference.* Grand Rapids: Baker Books, 2002.

This book covers both the theoretical and the practical: making the theological and societal case for churches to get involved in holistic ministry, as well as providing practical advice on how to develop a vision, form an organization, and develop partnerships.

Skjegstad, Joy. *Starting a Nonprofit at Your Church.* Herndon, VA: Alban Institute, 2002.

A comprehensive guide for congregations that want to develop separate 501(c)3 organizations, a step your church may want to consider if you are serious about attracting grant funding. The book covers the legal process, vision and mission, board issues, fundraising, human resources, and a number of other topics, all focused on the unique aspects of the church-based nonprofit.

Stockdill, Stacey Hueftle. *How to Evaluate Foundation Programs.* Golden Valley, MN: Ensearch, Inc., 1998.

This booklet offers step-by-step instructions for developing a program evaluation process, focusing mainly on developing data-collection methods such as questionnaires and focus groups. A number of concrete examples demonstrate in detail how to use these evaluation tools in a nonprofit setting.

Working Group on Human Needs and Faith-Based and Community Initiatives. *Finding Common Ground: 29 Recommendations of the Working Group on Human Needs and Faith-Based and Community Initiatives.* Washington, D.C.: Search for Common Ground, 2002.

The Working Group on Human Needs and Faith-Based and Community Initiatives is a project of Search for Common Ground, an organization working to transform the way people deal with conflict. The working group put together a report of 29 recommendations "to increase the capacity and effectiveness of community and faith-based organizations in meeting human needs." To read the full report, go to www.sfcg.org/programmes/us/report.pdf." Parts of this report are included in appendix 2 of this book. The report includes the two typologies of faith-based organizations referenced in chapter 5 of this book.

Web sites

www.boardsource.org

Everything you wanted to know about nonprofit boards and more! I like the FAQs (frequently asked questions) section of this Web site in particular.

www.fastennetwork.org

This is the Web site of the Faith and Service Technical Education Network (FASTEN). It is a rich resource on a variety of topics involving ministry development and nonprofit management. There are some great tips on grantwriting in the fundraising section, including information on how to find out about government grant opportunities. I also like the research on faith and philanthropy in the "Relationships" section.

www.guidestar.org

Guidestar features information on more than 1.5 million IRS-recognized nonprofits in the U.S. The basic level of Guidestar allows you to look at the 990-PF form for any IRS-recognized foundation, which provides information on the assets, grant-making activities, and officers and directors of each organization. You can register for the basic level of Guidestar for free, but there is a fee for the "fancier" search and data tools available on the Web site. The 990 form is a useful tool because it lists all of the grants made by the foundation in the previous year. If you are researching a funder that doesn't publish its list of grantees, the 990 form allows you to review the types of organizations funded and the amounts given to each.

www.nacba.net

The Web site for the National Association of Church Business Administration provides practical advice on a wide range of management issues for churches. NACBA does a salary survey on a regular basis and also provides resources on facilities management, insurance, legal and human resources issues, and a host of other topics. NACBA is a national organization with local chapters throughout the U.S.